Welcome to

Splice

I'm writing this editorial in spring 2013, just a few days before local council elections across large parts of the UK (although not where I live). The media story of these elections has been the emergence of the UK Independence Party (UKIP) as a viable contender for a substantial number of seats on the back of a couple of by-election performances where they finished second ahead of two of the 'mainstream' parties in each case. The Westminster Village wisdom is that, of the major political parties, the Conservatives have most to lose from UKIP's emergence, with its reliance on anti-Europe/immigration feeling, a rather ugly consequence of the economy showing few signs of waking from the coma of the last few years. I record this here not to launch my own political manifesto ('What do we want?' 'Media education!') but to note that it would be a uniquely naïve observer who did not take account of the timing of the (Conservative) Home Secretary Chris Grayling's latest public pronouncement about the UK's prisoner population. He intends to 'clamp down' on such 'perks' as Sky TV, the prison gym and – I'm not making this up – 18 certificate films. So all those body-conscious MPs banged-up for fiddling their expenses who are partial to Sky Atlantic and Ken Loach films (all that swearing!) are in for a jolly rough ride.

My point is that as the electoral clock ticks inexorably towards polling day it is noticeable just how often the issue of prisons (and, more abstractly, 'justice') gets dragged back into the open for a good hosing down by politicians and commentators. England and Wales have the highest per capita prison population in western Europe and yet rather than try to grapple with this, frankly, alarming situation, our political masters seem content to ignore it on a day-to-day basis, only bringing the subject up near an election when they want to be seen to be 'getting tough' – which, in Mr Grayling's case, appears to constitute turning off the telly.

Which is all by way of introducing the prison movies issue of Splice, one that covers the gamut of cinema from The Most Popular Film of All Time (if you believe IMDb and its users) to US indie and UK 'art cinema'. Hopefully you'll find something herein that serves as a deterrent to all those corruptible minds that teachers come into contact with on a daily basis. And if you are unsuccessful in keeping them on the straight and narrow, at least they'll be able to pass their incarceration reflecting on the time they discussed the representation of prison life in *American History X*. Although of course they won't be able to watch it inside, as it's an 18.

Lights out!

John Atkinson
Editor, *Splice*
splice@auteur.co.uk

From top: Susan Sarandon, Dead Man Walking*; Tom Hanks and Michael Clarke Duncan,* The Green Mile*; Sean Penn in* Dead Man Walking

Last Things:

The Dramatisation of the Death Penalty in the Popular Film

by James Clarke

Steve Earle, the American singer-songwriter, has written and performed songs about Death Row for some years. It's a setting and a subject that unsettles, upsets and enrages and, over a period of decades, popular film has dramatised the experience of the death penalty in a number of vivid ways. Earle's song 'Ellis Unit One' (heard on the soundtrack to *Dead Man Walking* (1995) and written from the perspective of a Death Row guard) includes the following verse:

> Well, folks just got too civilized /
> Sparky's gathering dust /
> 'Cause no one wants to touch a smokin' gun /
> And since they got the injection /
> They don't mind as much, I guess /
> They just put 'em down at Ellis Unit One.[1]

Earle's perceptive and necessarily melancholy and damning lyrics encapsulate a kind of response that we might recognise in the feature films that are discussed in this article.

To sketch out an age-old pattern very lightly, drama builds its scaffold on the terra-firma of conflict, where the forces of heart, mind, action and circumstance move in opposition to each other. Subsequently, chaos disrupts order and there then follows a concerted effort to restore the balance and return to what was known (or, in Todorovian terms, equilibrium-disorder-restored/new equilibrium). When this condition is eventually achieved there's typically an adjustment in characters' circumstance, perception and understanding. These are some of the expectations that we have cultivated about what a story (in movies, literature and song) can offer and certainly, the setting of a prison makes for a particularly concentrated arena in which these conventions and patterns of drama can play out.

Arguably, films can't change society... but... *but*...they *can* cast a light on difficult subjects and provide the spark from which the flame of larger discussion, and the wish to explore further, can grow. Importantly, films can sensitise viewers to points of view and experience outside of their own typical and familiar frames of reference. A film viewing, then, can play its part in prompting a newfound interest or awareness, at least, of a reality beyond the fairly closed realm that most of us live within.

Several years ago I wrote, here in *Splice* (Volume 1 issue 3, 2007), about some of the relationships to be identified between citizenship and film, and it's fair to say that, to some degree, this essay returns to that territory. In terms of what might guide us in considering citizenship and its relation to film we can look to the work of Andrew Burn (of the Centre for Media and Youth) who has indicated that (cine)literacy occurs in three contexts that are distinct and interrelated: cultural, critical (taste, pleasure judgements) and creative. Furthermore, Burn has explored how film-viewing nurtures our recognition of the powerful relationship between words and images. All of these considerations play their part in informing our range of responses to the films we'll look at in this piece.

The Maelstrom of Death Row: Condemnation and Compassion

Alarmingly, as the American writer Wendell Berry points out in his book of essays, *Art of the Commonplace*, there are now more prisoners than farmers in the world.[2] In America it's the case that 'Congress or any state legislature may prescribe the death penalty...'.[3] However, the American court system is required to 'consider the evolving standards of decency to determine if a particular punishment constitutes a cruel or unusual punishment'[4] Clearly, the subject of capital punishment is complex, challenging and can be depended on to quickly stir an emotional response. As I write this, a recent edition of the programme *Any Questions* on BBC Radio 4 (September 21st 2012) is fresh in my mind and a briefly held debate unfolded about the likelihood and wisdom (or ignorance) of reinstating the Death Penalty in Great Britain. It is, to my mind, a chilling prospect.

Some of you might recall the scene late in *Raging Bull* (Martin Scorsese, 1980) when Jake La Motta (Robert De Niro) punches, with his bare fists, relentlessly at a wall of the prison cell he has been placed in. Of this moment, and the choices made in realising it for the film, Martin Scorsese noted:

> I think it's the old story of having to reach the lowest level with yourself. It became a really collaborative experience, all of us working together. Bob slamming his head against the wall that way seemed to have the most power. As did his expression, "I'm not an animal. *I'm still human, I'm still human.*" What he meant, I think, is an animal doesn't have consciousness, is not aware that's it's alive. You're a much more complicated creature that just an animal.[5]

This attempt to use drama to humanise people who might easily otherwise have been demonized characterises the three films discussed in detail in this article.

Certainly, there's an extensive catalogue of prison-set films and they include titles such as *The Passion of Joan of Arc* (1928), *Scum* (1979), *La Grande Illusion* (1937), *The Great Escape* (1963), *Pickpocket* (1959), *Escape from Alcatraz* (1979), *Brubaker* (1980). For the contemporary audience perhaps *The Shawshank Redemption* (1994) is the most well-known, and resonant, prison movie of all. Of this film, Mark Kermode wrote, in his monograph, that 'For those who want to find them, there are indeed ample religious motifs woven into the fabric of *The Shawshank Redemption*'[6]. Indeed, prison-set stories are rich with possibilities for symbolism and metaphor.

When I was a postgraduate student at film school my final project was a drama piece realised in the TV studio production space for which we constructed a prison cell set. For research, in pursuit of some very modest claim to authenticity, we visited the police station in Bristol city centre, where, for just about half a minute, I had myself locked in a cell to get some sense of the loneliness, isolation and finality that must hang in the air of that small space. Thirty seconds was plenty of time in which for me to experience those senses. (Incidentally, and, forgive the name-dropping, one of the actors we cast in that student film was a then-unknown young actor named Idris Elba.) That sense of enclosure, and of closure, that I experienced are amongst the feelings and sensations that prison films have dramatised so potently; the focus and unity of time and place offered by the setting of a prison cell is Aristotelian in its dramatic potential.

Capital punishment and the difficult reality of Death Row are intensely powerful subjects engulfed by a maelstrom of ideas and responses around violence, revenge, law, religion, culture and race. Amnesty International has described the death penalty thus: 'The death penalty is the ultimate denial of human rights. It is the premeditated and cold-blooded killing of a human being by the state. This cruel, inhuman and degrading punishment is done in the name of justice.'[7]

In this piece I'd like to explore how three films (all produced over the last twenty years) dramatise the ramifications and act of capital punishment using cinematic devices to manipulate our response. It's dramatic because it provides a ticking clock for the drama to count down towards. Each of these films offers expression of ideas of justice and revenge, and our paradoxical capacities for both violence and compassion of thought and of action.

The films that we'll consider have specifically American and British settings and in each example, to varying degrees, the place of religious faith pertains to a significant part of the drama in recreating the moment of execution. In his book *Transcendental Style in Film*, Paul Schrader writes in detail about *The Passion of Joan of Arc* commenting that Joan is presented by the film's director, Carl Theodor Dreyer, as 'reactive to her social surroundings...the crucified, sacrificial lamb'.[8] I think we might say that each of the prisoners in the films discussed below await their respective executions in ways that echo the presentation of Joan.

Dead Man Walking (Tim Robbins, 1995)

We approach *Dead Man Walking* as a realistic movie, which is to say as a movie that seeks to play down its inevitable artifice. In a sense we might say that it's a film without an evident style and yet when we pay closer attention to just a portion of the material you'll recognise how its engineering of story is so fully and deliberately accomplished. This precise construction is common to all films, and it's the smart thing to be mindful of this in terms of those films that look like they don't have a 'style'. For example, the films directed by Ken Loach and John Sayles films might appear to be without style or artifice but they have their own structures and patterns. Don't forget that style *is* substance – a truth that's perhaps easier to identify and investigate in the more overtly patterned or designed films of directors such as Ridley Scott, Christopher Nolan, Wes Anderson and Martin Scorsese, to name just a few film-makers popular with students. To paraphrase film director Jean-Luc Godard: style is the outside of content and content is the inside of style. By extension, it's useful to remember, too, that aesthetics and ethics have a deep connection.

Dead Man Walking is a film whose drama is informed by an actual (that is, real life) relationship that developed between a convicted murderer named Matthew

Poncelet (Sean Penn) and a nun, Sister Helen Prejean (Susan Sarandon), who visited him regularly in the months leading to his execution. Subsequently, Sister Prejean wrote a memoir of her encounter entitled *Dead Man Walking: An Eye Witness Account of the Death Penalty in the United States*. The book placed Sister Prejean into the public arena and she has made the powerful point that 'I'm facing a culture that legitimizes murder as vengeance'.[9]

Of the film's conception, its director Tim Robbins, in conversation with Charlie Rose during promotion for the film's theatrical release, noted that:

> I wanted to open the door, you know. It's a very serious thing, you know, that we're doing, killing people, and if we can't look in that door and see the specifics of what really happens, there's something wrong. So basically what we're doing is, in an honest way, presenting both sides of the issue and looking inside the door of the death chamber, and we're trying to reflect reality in there. I think what's interesting about the reaction is that, is that people are coming away sometimes with the same opinion as when they went in, but that's okay. It's good that they're talking about it. If we're going to do such a serious thing, we should at least be able to talk about it.[10]

In these comments, Robbins attests to popular film's capacity to offer a way into discussions of seemingly abstract or difficult subjects. Spielberg's *Schindler's List* (1993) performed a similar function.

We'll focus here on the execution scene in *Dead Man Walking*. Consistent with the film as a whole, for the most part, the sequence adopts a realist strategy, but is more pointedly manipulative, or artificial, at moments. The scene, which lasts about ten minutes, begins with a close up of Sister Helen and then cuts to a close up of Matthew who is sitting, crying behind the bars of his cell. The shot holds for half a minute (a long time for a single shot) and this sense of real time passing is compelling, forcing the viewer to confront the situation the drama refers to.

There is then a shot of Helen watching as the families of Poncelet's victims gather to watch his execution. The camera then pans from Helen to show us Matthew being led from his cell. The camera pan connects the spaces of public and prisoner in a way that a cut would inevitably not. There is then a cut to Matthew shaking and Helen says quietly to him 'When they do this thing you look at me'. Helen's use of the word 'thing' speaks of the absurdity (of the worst kind) of the process and also speaks to the way in which the event is beyond understanding through words. Sure enough, it's the images that soon follow that communicate the awfulness of the act.

Sister Helen's expression of compassionate love for Matthew is interrupted by the prison guard who brusquely explains that it's 'Time to go, Poncelet'. Significantly, the shot holds on Sister Helen in close up and we only hear the guard's voice, keeping him non-specific and therefore allowing his voice to represent the voice and institution of authority more generally. Sister Helen's reaction is guiding our reaction.

Matthew's execution – *Dead Man Walking*

We become aware of mournful choral music being introduced on the soundtrack and there is a medium wide shot of Poncelet being finally led away from Sister Helen, the shot concluding with a guard coming to the foreground, almost entirely occupying the screen, albeit momentarily, as he shouts the phrase 'Dead Man Walking' (the rather chilling tradition of prison guards announcing that a prisoner is being taken to their execution). There is then a cut to a slow motion shot (a stylistic choice on the director's part that explicitly rejects realism) of Matthew's slippered feet, followed by a shot of his waist where we see that he is wearing a nappy (for practical purposes but it also has the effect of infantilizing the prisoner). There is then another slow motion shot of Matthew as he closes his eyes. Again, this fleeting moment of heightened realism communicates the potential meaning and resonance of the image.

There is a cut to Sister Helen looking at Matthew and, critically, at this point the sequence has been stripped of *all* diegetic sync-sound so that all we hear is the non-diegetic music. As such, it's a moment of high auditory artifice, set against the 'realism' of the apparently unaffected image. There is then a cut that restores the sync sound (realistic) as Helen, walking at Matthew's side, the people tightly packed in around him recalling the crush of faces around Christ in the painting *Christ Carrying the Cross* (painted c.1515) by Hieronymous Bosch, reads from the Bible, declaring 'Do not be afraid'.

There is then a shot in which the camera tracks in towards a priest who speaks a brief blessing for Matthew before a guard again interrupts (brutally overwhelming a moment of compassion), saying 'That's as far as you go, Sister'.

A shot follows in which the camera tilts up to show Poncelet being strapped down on a bed and there is a close up that captures the moment when one of the straps is pulled across his wrists, evoking the image of nails hammered into Christ's hands. In the next close up the camera holds on a needle (the lethal injection – the mode of execution) going into Poncelet's arm and then pans to his face. This choice of a pan is important as it shows that the actor Penn has himself had his arm actually pierced by a needle for the performance. It's a moment when the actor's 'committed' performance is as significant as the reality of the character and larger situation that he portrays. (Because *Dead Man Walking* is based on a true story and restages actual events, to what extent might it be considered 'a documentary'?)

There is then a cut to a wide shot taken from within the public viewing gallery, which is attached to the execution chamber. A curtain is pulled aside to finally show the sinister spectacle of Poncelet on the raised bed, his arms outstretched, readily associating, for some of us, with the image of Christ crucified. Matthew asks for forgiveness and there is then a wide shot of Sister Helen looking at him and we see Matthew's reflection in the glass that divides the gallery from the execution chamber. There is an extreme close up on Helen's tearful eyes and Matthew's final moments are intercut with shots of the rape and murder for which he has been put to death. Music underscores this segment, a low-end hum combined with a wailing kind of lament.

In this sequence, faith, punishment and a visualized, rather than verbalised critique of the medieval barbarity of capital punishment finds expression. In turn, the film lends expression to what we might call the spiritual, by which we might really mean the deepest, more fundamental sense a person has of themselves in relation to the world. The American critic Roger Ebert enthused thus: 'For years, critics have asked for more films that deal with the spiritual side of life. I doubt if *Dead Man Walking* was what they were thinking of, but this is exactly how such a movie looks, and feels.'[11]

Let Him Have It (Peter Medak, 1991)

Let Him Have It is constructed powerfully from the tradition of British cinema's impulse towards social realism. Before getting to the specifics of the film it's worth quoting, at some length, from the BFI's Screenonline resource about the dynamics of realism on screen:

...early British cinema picked up on the revelation of everyday social interaction to be found in Dickens and Thomas Hardy... In the years following World War I, it was widely felt that the key to a national cinema lay in 'realism and restraint'. Such a view reflected the tastes of a mainly south-eastern, middle-class audience. Meanwhile, working-class audiences, it was said, favoured Hollywood genre movies. So realism carried patrician connotations of education and high seriousness. These social and aesthetic distinctions have become running themes in a cinema for which social realism is now associated with the arthouse auteur, while 'entertainment' plays at the multiplex.[12]

The closing statement of this little bit of context is pertinent to *Let Him Have It* and also to *Dead Man Walking*. However, is it the case that *The Green Mile* (see below) falls more squarely into the category of 'entertainment'?

Let Him Have It is based on a real life event that occurred in 1952 in which two armed teenagers, attempting to burgle a warehouse, were confronted by police. The one teenager, Derek Bentley, shouted out to his friend Christopher Craig to 'Let him have it, Chris'. Craig took this to mean to shoot at the policeman they were confronted by and so fired. Sure enough, the case went to court and Craig and Bentley were both charged with murder. But it was Bentley who was hanged. The decision to hang Bentley was eventually overturned as a miscarriage of justice and served to accentuate how contentious the case had always been. Bentley had acknowledged learning difficulties and one could argue that in saying 'Let him have it' he meant for Craig hand the gun over. Bentley did not use either gun that he was carrying.

In the film, the sequence that revolves around Bentley's execution is not as sentimentally achieved as equivalent scenes in *Dead Man Walking* and *The Green Mile*. It is a very emotive sequence, though, trading more on silence. But in common with *Dead Man Walking* and *The Green Mile* the visuals communicate the barbarity of the death penalty, whether by hanging, lethal injection or electrocution.

The climactic sequence begins with a wide shot of Bentley (Christopher Ecclestone) positioned on the left of frame, sitting on cell bunk dictating a letter to the policeman sitting opposite him. It's an instance of kindness in the harshest, most desperate circumstances. Derek Bentley dictates details of looking after the pets, etc. There is then a cut to Derek's mother (Eileen Atkins) walking towards her house on a London suburban street. A large crowd has gathered outside her home and she walks through them, saying nothing. The sequence then cuts back to Derek in his cell and the camera zooms in slowly on him as he continues dictating his letter, saying that 'The truth of this story has got to come out one day'. The policeman has a certain kindness about him, contrasting with the prison guards' presentation in *Dead Man Walking* but comparing more favourably with most of the guards in *The Green Mile*. There is then another cut back to the family home and a sustained close up of Derek's mother, sister and father; the camera pans across each of their solemn faces as the clock ticking towards 9am and the moment of execution. This attenuated moment recalls a similar shot early in the sequence we've considered from *Dead Man Walking*. There is then a cut that takes the action of the sequence out to the road and we watch Derek's father (Tom Courtenay) step out. In the wide shot we see the postman approach and hand him just one letter. The camera then pulls up and away from the house as plaintive piano music plays on the soundtrack, a musical motif that will bind together the next few shots.

The sequence cuts back to Derek, this time shown in a medium close up with the camera at a low height looking up at him in the foreground as a priest stands behind him in the background reading out the Lord's Prayer. There is then a cut to an overhead shot of the family in the front room of their terraced house. There is no dialogue to be heard here, only the sound of the ticking clock and the piano playing on the soundtrack. On the mantelpiece in a successive shot in which the family embraces each other we see two candles alight, suggesting a connection to religion and light in darkness. From the tableau there is a cut to the camera tracking hard in on the clock and there is then a cut to a crowd of Bentley's supporters outside the prison holding banners proclaiming Bentley's innocence as the people sing the hymn 'Abide With Me'. There is then a cut to a mid-shot that shows Derek sitting at a table when he is interrupted by the incursion of prison guards who order him to stand and drink, the mechanics of the execution now being put into practice. It's not dissimilar to the insensitive moment of the prison guard in *Dead Man Walking*. A guard approaches the camera and

  raises the hood towards us, just starting to cover the lens, a point of view shot that vividly putting us in Bentley's shoes. There is even a tracking shot along a line of men who are legally obliged to witness the hanging. Bentley's tie is removed and a series of quick cuts show us Bentley removing his shoes and then having his hands bound. There is then a shot that rhymes with a similar image in *Dead Man Walking* of Derek walking towards the gallows and into close up.

A wide shot then coldly shows the gallows floor panel giving way and Derek being hanged. It's an unfussily presented moment, as stark as can be, the absence of a further close up on Bentley perhaps denying us the expected moment of more emphatic emotional connection to the victim. It also avoids something potentially more sentimental. This austerely rendered shot is then followed by a shot of overt artifice in which the camera tracks up the rope and the screen briefly whites out.

The Green Mile (Frank Darabont, 1999)

Like *Dead Man Walking*, *The Green Mile* is based on a published source and set in the American South in the twentieth century. Unlike *Dead Man Walking*, the source is a novel from one of the world's most popular genre writers, Stephen King. Perhaps inevitably, King's identity as a horror novelist is not far from our minds as we approach the film. But we find that this story tones down his more elaborate horrors and monstrosities to something very real-world in its grotesquerie: the process of Death Row and the shadow that hangs over its prisoners *and* jailers.

More overtly than *Dead Man Walking* or *Let Him Have It*, *The Green Mile* demonstrates a Gothic sensibility. This does *not* mean that the film is replete with vampires or castles (although a nocturnal exterior shot of the prison under rainy, stormy skies fleetingly suggests such a place) but instead it's a broader description of tone and story. Indeed, the values of the Gothic, of heightened reality, are qualities that characterise aspects of *The Green Mile* and even connect with those in the work of Charles Dickens, the popularity and standing of whom we might equate with that of Stephen King – who, perhaps not co-incidentally, originally published *The Green Mile* in serial form, just as Dickens' novels first appeared in the nineteenth century. Like King, and like the Hollywood storytelling machine, Dickens applied genre tropes to 'social' subjects. Here's Dickens himself, in a rare moment of reflection on his own attitude towards writing process, elaborating on his interest in the storytelling potential of the Gothic. Is it fair to say that we can see how a line could be traced from the popular nineteenth century novelist to the twentieth century popular film-maker?

It does not seem to me to be enough to say of any description of a tone and sensibility that it is the exact truth. The exact truth must be there; but the merit or art in the narrator, is the manner of stating the truth. As to which is literature, it always seems to me that there is a world to be done. And in these times, when the tendency is to be frightfully literal and catalogue-like – to make the thing, in short, a sort of sum in reduction that any miserable creature can do in that way – I have an idea (really founded on the love of what I profess), that the very holding of popular literature through a kind of popular dark age, may depend on such fanciful treatment.[13]

Enhancing the sense that Dickens is getting at about the act of 'treating' reality, we can turn to the work of scholar Robert Mighall. In his essay 'Defining the Gothic' he notes that 'The Gothic is obsessed with the historical past and how this affects the present'[14]. Certainly, Mighall's plainly-spoken description touches on fundamentals of the realities being dramatised in the films discussed here.

In approaching the dark subject matter, Frank Darabont, the screenwriter and director of *The Green Mile* film and also of the other famous Stephen King prison adaptation, *The Shawshank Redemption*, drew an analogy to the story of Christ and we might say with some confidence that each film discussed here expresses, to varying degrees, some connection to Christian imagery. Most interestingly though, in relation to *The Green Mile*, it was actor Michael Jeter (who plays Eduard Delacroix) who made the most affecting observation, when he noted that for the actors the film was about 'playing people who are dealing with last things'[15]. It's a melancholy assessment which also underpins *Dead Man Walking* and *Let Him Have It*.

The Green Mile charts life on death row for the prisoners and their guards at Cold Mountain prison. The action parses the relations between the guards and the men behind bars, most significantly John Coffey (Michael Clarke Duncan), the imposing but gentle black man who has been found guilty of murdering two young white girls.

I'd like to briefly focus now on a sequence that offers a peak moment of drama, right in the middle of the film: it's the sequence that depicts the execution of Del, a man fragile of both mind and body. For many films, it's the scenes that occur midway through their respective running times that often provide an opportunity to encapsulate some of the sensibilities of the movie as a whole. In the case of *The Green Mile*, the sequence showing Del's execution draws together the film's expressions of cruelty and of kindness.

The sequence begins with an exterior shot, relishing in the chance to conjure melodramatically thunderous skies and lightning flashes that perhaps have more in common with movie stylins and generic convention than with a more meteorologically inclined vibe, but the intensity rightly amplifies the drama and sense of impending doom. As such, we are reminded that *The Green Mile* is, at least in part, a horror film, offering producers and audience an opportunity to dwell on some of those things that we might typically push aside and repress.

From the wide-shot of the stormy exterior of the prison the sequence then cuts to an interior setting, Del's cell on 'the Green Mile', as a close up shows us Mr Jingles the mouse cradled in Del's hands. The camera tilts up to momentarily hold a profile shot of Del (Michael Jeter) in a moment of repose. The scene then cuts to a wide-shot that shows Del on his bed on the right of frame whilst the background is dominated by the gathering of the prison guards, led by Paul Edgecomb (Tom Hanks) and 'Brutal' Howell (David Morse). Del comes out to the men and, given the action that is about to unfold, the scene is marked by the evident warmth between prisoner and prison guards: 'You're a good man,' Del says to Brutal, and then adds 'I sure wish I could have met you guys someplace else'. Del then hands his mouse, Mr Jingles, to Paul and when it's clear that he doesn't want to look after it John Coffey's voice is heard saying that he'll care for the mouse. It seems a fairly innocuous offer at this moment.

Del is then walked away, the sense of emotional enormity being visualised with a cut to a shot from above the floor of the the Green Mile as Del is escorted along it.

The action then cuts to the well-attended execution chamber, the grotesquerie of it recalling the similar, more clinically organised and modern setting of the venue that features in *Dead Man Walking*. One of the witnesses for Del's execution takes evident pleasure in the occasion, saying that they 'hope he's good and scared'.

Thomas Newman's delicate score emphasises the moment when Del is brought into the room and then strapped into the electric chair, the camera tilting up from his wrists to his face. As with *Dead Man Walking* there's an acknowledgement here that it really is the actor who is being strapped into the chair. The realism of the circumstances of the performance are important to the believability of the drama and its mounting tension.

The action then cuts back to the Green Mile and to John Coffey (Michael Clarke Duncan) in his cell. We only see a close up of Coffey's immense hands cupping Mr Jingles: 'You be so quiet,' he says to the mouse, a moment of gentleness so acutely counterpointing the state-sanctioned violence occurring simultaneously. In another cell Wild Bill (Sam Rockwell) manically enthuses about the execution of Del as the sequence continues to build through a frenzy of intercutting action between the execution chamber, Wild Bill and John Coffey. We then see another shot of Coffey's hands and the camera then tilts up to his face which registers his distress. As the scene builds there is then a close up on Coffey's hands as he cries out 'Del!' The bulbs in the lights on the Green Mile explode as Coffey absorbs Del's suffering. In a sense it's a far more melodramatic, and sensational, moment that parallels Helen Prejean's absorption of Matthew's suffering in *Dead Man Walking*.

There is then a close up of Del's hands clenched on the arms of the execution chair as he writhes in the moment of execution and the sequence then cuts back to John Coffey's hands, clenched on his knees, the images echoing each other; the connection between John and Del made clear, just as, albeit rather less melodramatically, the editing pattern in the execution scene of *Dead Man Walking* constructed a spiritual connection (of compassion) between Matthew and Sister Helen.

Throughout *The Green Mile* there are scenes that turn on the issue of how to treat each other; in effect, the scenes ask, what is it to behave with decency and goodness in conditions that would seem to utterly negate them?

Ahead of his own execution, Coffey asks to watch a film and the guards screen a Fred Astaire and Ginger Rogers film. Coffey describes Astaire and Rogers as being like angels. The film is *Top Hat* (1935) and is a romantic comedy that we might say gives expression to the good that people can embody towards each other. A close up of John watching the film frames him with the projector beam radiating in the darkness behind him and lending him a halo of sorts.

The film is about mortality as the head guard Paul deals with his own aging and the necessary schism between professional duty and personal affection for Coffey. Contrasting with Paul's sensitivity to the work at hand is an early scene in which Paul and prison Warden Hal Moores (James Cromwell) discuss the guard Percy Wetmore (Doug Hutchison) and his 'sheer petulance' in terms of an assault made on a prisoner. Wetmore shows no respect for the prisoners, functioning as the caricature of the insensitive prison guard – the worst version of the authority figures we see in a more allusive way in *Dead Man Walking* and *Let Him Have It*.

Perhaps the most chilling scene in *The Green Mile* occurs when the guards stage a routine execution rehearsal. This scene, I think, really gets at the inhuman practice of the death penalty much more so than the scenes that show prisoners actually being executed. They stage it with Toots the cleaner (Harry Dean Stanton) as a stand-in for the doomed prisoner. It's a scene that reinforces the brutality and medieval nature of the punishment, with Toots joking and sneering about repentance as he willingly walks through the motions. In effect, Toots mocks the scenario and particularly the connection between Death Row, justice and God. At the film's climax and the execution of John Coffey, the scene certainly emphasises the ugliness of the mob who have come to gloat and, perhaps surprisingly, no musical underscore is used to additionally manipulate our feeling and thought.

The film's larger consideration of 'why bad things happen' is addressed in a scene in which Paul visits Burt Hammersmith (Gary Sinise), the lawyer who defended Coffey even though he was sure of his guilt. Hammersmith's facial expression never registers more than a certain muted anger and steeliness. There's no room for a smile or the glimmer of uncertainty or ambiguity about Coffey. The scene includes several cut-aways to Hammersmith's children playing which seems arbitrary until the scene's conclusion. Hammersmith is deeply cautious about human nature – there's a first time for everything is Hammersmith's mantra. Paul has gone to Burt to see if Coffey really did commit the crime: 'There doesn't seem to be any violence in him', Paul contends. But Hammersmith takes a different view that insists upon the primacy of the legal process rather than a deeper, more humanistic sensibility.

Conclusion

Ultimately, despite our sincerity in wanting to think about how something as apparently commonplace as a film can alert us to a much more serious subject, and give expression to the idea of decency at work in a cruel world, one rather large quandary sits right next to us as we watch these films. If entertainment is about escape from reality and the spirit of 'fun', how can the recreation of such torment be considered entertaining? Is it, in fact a very insensitive thing to do; ultimately cheapening what remains the fact of the death penalty in many parts of the world? Is there some degree of titillation inherent beneath the camouflage of 'social comment'? It's a difficult question to untangle as, in the same breath, we recognise that the films we've been considering can genuinely move the viewer, if only for a moment, towards new lines of thought and understanding about a subject they'd perhaps never otherwise care to consider.

Bibliography/references

1. Steve Earle, 'Ellis Unit One', *Dead Man Walking* soundtrack and also on the album *Sidetracks* by Steve Earle
2. Wendell Berry, *The Art of the Commonplace*, Counterpoint Press
3. Cornell Law website: http://www.law.cornell.edu/wex/death_penalty
4. Cornell Law website: www.law.cornell.edu/wex/death-penalty
5. Martin Scorsese, quoted by Richard Schickel in *Conversations with Scorsese*, Knopf, 2011
6. Mark Kermode, www.guardian.co.uk/film/2004/aug/22/film
7. Amnesty International, http://www.amnesty.org/en/death-penalty
8. Paul Schrader, *Transcendental Style In Film: Ozu, Bresson, Dreyer*, Da Capo Press, 1988: 121
9. Helen Prejean, http://www.sisterhelen.org/justice-lost-in-drive-for-vengeance/
10. Tim Robbins, http://www.pbs.org/wgbh/pages/frontline/angel/walking/timrobbins.html
11. Roger Ebert, http://rogerebert.suntimes.com/apps/pbcs.dll/article?AID=/19960112/REVIEWS/601120301/1023
12. BFI Screenonline, http://www.screenonline.org.uk/film/id/1037898/index.html
13. Charles Dickens, quoted in the Introduction to *Charles Dickens: Selected Short Fiction*, edited by Deborah A. Thomas, Penguin Classics, 1987: 14
14. Robert Mighall, *Defining the Gothic*, from *A Companion to Charles Dickens*, edited by David Paroissien, Blackwell Publishing, 2008: 82
15. Michael Jeter, quoted from interview in *Walking the Mile* documentary on *The Green Mile* DVD, Warner Bros Home Video.

Missing an issue?

Volume 1 issue 3 (2007)
Sin City and *A History of Violence*; using *Star Wars* to teach Citizenship; *An Inconvenient Truth*

Volume 3 issue 1 (2008) – Crime film special
Minority Report and science fiction noir; French crime film; using film noir to introduce Film Studies

Volume 3 issue 2 (2009) – Green onscreen
introducing eco-themes with Film and Media Studies; horror cinema and landscape; cinema and wilderness

Volume 3 issue 3 (2009)
Boys Don't Cry; the *Red Riding* TV series; *Bullet Boy*

Volume 6 issue 1 (2012)
Documentary special
Star directors and the modern documentary; Werner Herzog; war documentaries since 9/11; *Catfish*

Volume 6 issue 2 (2012)
Sports and Games issue
The Hunger Games; the sports films of Will Ferrell; screening the Olympics; *Moneyball*

You may have forgotten to renew your subscription one year, or perhaps have started teaching an area that was covered by an earlier issue of *Splice* (could be recent British cinema, animation, crime film or short films). Individual back copies of *Splice* are available direct from Auteur at £14.99 plus p+p. Go to www.auteur.co.uk and click on 'Books' to pull up the 'Splice' tab, where you will find a full list of back issues; or contact us at splice@auteur.co.uk to see if we have the issue you need.

The Running Mann:

The *Jericho Mile* and Folsom Prison

by Deryck Swan

When I was in the ring at the Olympics, it was my father's words that I was hearing, not the coaches'. I never listened to what the coaches said. I would call my father and he would give me advice from prison. Floyd Mayweather, Jr

The Jericho Mile

In *The Jericho Mile* (1979), Michael Mann's TV Movie of the Week debut, prison is indeed a place of sage words and life lessons. It is a film that shares some commonalities with his future work but is more interesting (and more frustrating) because of its seeming departures from the tropes that would come into play with *Thief* (1981) - also known as *Violent Streets* in the US - and those related films beyond. This essay will deal with this intriguing interplay of like and difference that *Jericho* offers up and we shall start with the most useful thing that it provided Mann with – Folsom Prison itself.

Ostensibly the most salient aspect of *The Jericho Mile* that must be lain across a large tract of Mann's career is the idea of prison culture as a formative force in the lives of criminals. Mann's time working within the walls of Folsom Prison as a writer on *Straight Time* (1978), Dustin Hoffman's movie adaptation of Eddie Bunker's all time great prison novel *No Beast So Fierce*, allowed him to acquire an intimate understanding of the culture and cadence of prison life, specifically West Coast (and, to an extent, Midwest) prison culture, as exemplified here by Folsom and later by the penitentiaries of Chino, Joliet, McNeil and Statesville. It became apparent to Mann while working on *Straight Time* that Folsom and its sister institutions were of a specific kind, a breed apart where there existed a kind of counterintuitive orderliness to life inside precisely because of their extreme notoriety. Because these prisons were regarded as end-of-the-line institutions, where inmates with long sentences or violent histories would end up as a last resort in their custodial lives, Mann realised that those same prisons often played an important part in shaping the convicts' philosophies about the future and how they should conduct themselves in life. This confluence of certain breeds of criminal would then result in the formation of a kind of distorted criminal graduate school, where the inmates could acquire or refine skills that would then service their later careers in robbery or homicide or, in the case of 'Rain' Murphy (Peter Strauss) in *The Jericho Mile*, distance running. As an extension of character and a manifestation of professionalism, the running that Murphy chooses to define himself by in *Jericho* is no different than the safe cracking chosen by Frank in Thief or the bank robbery chosen by Neil McCauley in *Heat* (1995). All are activities learned and perfected *in prison* because of the way that these institutions impact on the criminal and force the mind into this very myopic pursuit of self-determination. Such a notion of prison, as something that actively promotes the kind of high line professionalism that holds sway in much of Mann's work, is something that has its genesis in *The Jericho Mile* and its view of Folsom.

The self-determining professionalism that's present in Murphy through his Olympic running in *Jericho* colours his whole approach to serving out his sentence in Folsom. The film's central expression of his sagacity and stoicism perhaps shares some undercurrents with the mythos of the Chicago underworld of the 1930s and '40s, when Mann was growing up and learning about those career professionals like Dillinger and Lamm, men dedicated to being the best at what they did. In a way, *The Jericho Mile* is Mann's first motion picture exploration of this prototype criminal male that he would go on to investigate again and again, through the opiate of the 1980s aesthetic of *Thief* and, to a lesser extent, *Manhunter* (1986), the 90s anti-capitalism of *Heat* and the bold 30s recidivism of *Public Enemies* (2009) – experts all defined by a philosophy of work moulded and shaped in prison. Although *Jericho* is the only Michael Mann film where the protagonist is actually in jail (in *Public Enemies* Dillinger is in jail momentarily and only so that we can witness the thrill of him breaking out!), those other entries cited above still draw upon the indelible portent of prison, a place that must be both acknowledged by the main characters as the source of their skills and repudiated as a place never to be returned to. Look again at *Heat* and the way that prison has shaped McCauley's look and behaviour – the impossibly starched collar of the coffee shop meeting, the origami napkin he leaves around Eady's glass, the newspaper cuttings that hide his domestic life – or the way a forced return to prison hangs over his head throughout its running time, a stifling presence that threatens to nullify all his creative efforts to escape to the island paradise of New Zealand.

Crucially, where *The Jericho Mile* departs from this template is in its deeper characterisation of Murphy, the central figure, and of Folsom itself. Murphy, unlike Frank in *Thief* or Neil in *Heat* or Dillinger in *Public Enemies*, was not a career criminal before his incarceration and has no criminal aspirations beyond it. At the start of the film Murphy finds himself already in jail for the murder of his abusive father and is doing his time in strict adherence to a dictum of self-imposed solitude that exiles him from the 'normal' spectrum of prison experience. Murphy regards his imprisonment as a justified response to the murder of his father and, through his running, gains a kind of catharsis from his experiences there. The view Mann's criminal protagonists would later take, that of prison as a necessary learning curve in the beginning and an impediment to success later on, is completely absent here, replaced instead by this almost idealistic stance that Murphy has regarding his jail time and what it can give him. Murphy is resigned to his imprisonment and has adopted a mental attitude and a physical activity to endure it. The Folsom itself of *Jericho* is a place that, rather than inhibiting opportunity, provides it willingly. It is jail that affords Murphy the recognition of his true running ability. It is jail that facilitates his track time and general practice needed to qualify for his climactic Olympic bid. It is in jail that he breaks the 4-minute mile and, in doing so, transcends his past deeds. These aspects point to an odd naivety in the film, a naivety that runs (perhaps deliberately) against the film's bid for authenticity and realism, but is nevertheless very helpful in understanding *Jericho*'s overall uniqueness in Mann's canon. Despite the seriousness of the stories found in *The Jericho Mile* the environment of Folsom seems somewhat outlandish in what it permits Murphy to achieve.

The hi fi man

The film begins with a series of abstract images presenting the vagaries of experience to be found during a stint of yard time for the inmates at Folsom. One prisoner dances in time to the beat emanating from his handheld hi fi, a variant of the unmistakable sound of The Rolling Stones' 'Sympathy for the Devil' emerging from both his speakers *and* the soundtrack itself in a playful manipulation of the diegesis of the film. Still further images show inmates playing chess, lifting weights, styling one another's hair and, for Murphy and Stiles (Richard Lawson), running on the track. The discordant choice of music and the selection of these disconnected and subjective images establishes Folsom as an unknowable and highly individualised environment, a place where a clear establishing shot is never fully rendered for the benefit of the audience. This method of providing the viewer with fractions that represent the whole, of limiting the spatial understanding of a place and instead offering this smattering of disparate vignettes, is both an element crucial to understanding the politics of *The Jericho Mile* – and by extension what Murphy represents – and Mann's enduring project to deconstruct the conventional requirements of drama. The opening sequence offers an understanding of these facets willingly, particularly a glimpse into the politics of the age and the director. The montage has a freshness to it, a feel of quintessentially 1970s radicalism that chimes with the film's larger story of an inmate going it alone and empowering himself in time with the movements of emancipation and liberation that characterised the decade as a whole. The film will maintain this note of defiance right to the celebratory closing shots where Murphy ceremonially discards his stopwatch like Harry Callahan did with his police badge in 1971's *Dirty Harry*. Both are loaded gestures, acts of movie insubordination that bookend the tumultuous years between. Indeed the very first image of *Jericho*, the inmate bopping to the beats on his hi fi, has a definite dissenting quality to it as the inmate loses himself in a world of music and, as a result, gives the finger to the warden and the system that holds him. It's worth recalling that Mann himself used the opportunity to attend London International Film School in the late-1960s not only to learn how to wield a camera but also to avoid the draft for Vietnam, a conflict he, like Muhammad Ali, objected to and refused to validate by signing up for. *The Jericho Mile* capitalises on this conscientious objection and can be viewed, beyond itself, as a run through of some of the ideas and character traits that Mann would condense, most potently, into *Ali* (2001).

The shots of Murphy running in these opening minutes hint towards an idea that will be quickly developed as the story takes hold, namely that this character deliberately insulates himself from the gamut of normal social experiences on the yard because of the guilt he feels for killing his father. This dedication to principled behaviour is something that, as we shall see, Mann often uses to both generate sympathy for his criminal protagonists (because those principles are always assailed by an external force) and separate them from the more extreme criminals that are, to all intents and purposes, the conventional 'villains' of his films. This allows Mann to avoid any overt moralising with regards to the criminal activity undertaken by his protagonists – specifically bank robbery and high line burglary – because their acts are offset by the real criminals, the psychotic murderers and drug dealers who attract and deserve our judgement. These creations, the psychopaths like The Tooth Fairy in *Manhunter*, Mann's adaptation of Thomas Harris' *Red Dragon*, are rendered as the real criminals because they don't appeal to any precept of professional conduct that validates their actions and restrains their behaviour. Consider again how appealing Hannibal Lektor is made in *Manhunter*, how thrilling the reach from his cage is, how absolved he is of his past history, when placed against the psychopathology and chaos of Tom Noonan's lunar killer. Such is the extent of the moral relativism in Mann's evocation of crime and criminology, a framework that can be frustratingly ambiguous and yet also thrilling in its manipulation of audience sympathies and loyalties.

Some of the other principal characters of the film are introduced in these opening minutes including: Dr. D (played by Brian Dennehy), Folsom's resident drug king and the most *criminal* criminal of the film; Stiles, who here appears as Murphy's running mate and will later prove to be his counsel; and, most interestingly, Charlie Loon, played by the genuine Folsom convict Steven White, a true blue white supremacist both in the film and out whose character is used here by Dr. D to murder Stiles when he refuses to be extorted as a drug mule. The patina of prison life that is offered to the audience here evinces the odd notion of being both realistic and contrived at the same time. The sense of realism emerges from the identification of things like the racial gang structures within Folsom, the affiliations between the powerful, the modes of personal expression that include tattooing and the existence of a micro-economy founded on the illicit distribution of mostly drugs and pruno, an improvised alcoholic drink made in prison from things like ketchup. Most of the montage captures these details in static shots stitched together elliptically in a manner popularised during the 1970s by the likes of William Friedkin and Costa-Gavras who, in turn, borrowed from Truffaut and Godard. What's past is prologue indeed.

Counterposed against this verite feel is the emergence of a *style* that, while not distracting or definitive (this would not happen until Mann's next feature, *Thief*), nevertheless seems to impose itself on the material before us. Most notably, Mann's camera dollies around the African-American crew lifting weights and then Dr. D and his cronies, two very obvious camera *movements* that undermine the (seeming) candidness of the rest of this montage. Is this the first example of the tension that exists in some of Mann's films between style and realism? Like Martin Scorsese, most evidently in his 1973 calling card *Mean Streets* with its fusion of long lens street realism and red light barroom styling (Scorsese has always worn his love of Powell & Pressburger's *The Red Shoes* [1948] on his sleeve), Mann has often engaged in a balancing act of needing to tell narratives that are grounded in a form of street realism but that also look dreamy, even hallucinogenic, to the eye. The style imposed here by Mann, the smooth arcs around these groups of principal convicts, is not at all something that characterises him today (indeed it is a struggle to think of another of Mann's films that uses such a camera movement around its characters); what it does point to however is a small instance of direction, of the sense that there is a *personality* behind the events of the film, perhaps not a 'distinguishable' personality of the kind that Andrew Sarris required for entry to his auteur club, but a personality nonetheless. What this aspect of *Jericho*'s opening sequence shows is that Mann was already peeking above the parapet of pure (TV) narrative and offering a notion of creative agency to the savvy viewer, albeit a very marginal notion at this early stage.

Folsom's mural of death

The final element of *Jericho*'s minor prologue worth mentioning here is its splicing in of Folsom's mural artwork, specifically the work of Willie Heron III of *Los Illegals* fame. The celebratory bleakness of Heron's famous Folsom portrait of Death, here glimpsed in disparate fragments that build towards a full reveal of the skeletal figure dressed in a black hooded cloak and wielding what looks to be a staff of lightening and Christ's crown of thorns, both sums up the overall philosophy of many of these West Coast institutions – a kind of rigorous, violent, faith-based, tightly-structured nihilism – and reinforces the ultimate fate of many of their hard-line inmates; Murphy will die in Folsom despite his attempts to transcend its walls. Mann's love of street art and the inclusion of it in his films dealing with West Coast narratives is another key element in grasping his overall attempt to express the truer racial, social and political nature of this environment, particularly – as we shall see – the environment in and around Los Angeles, which is as important to understanding his view of modernity as Chicago is to understanding his view of crime.

The verite feel returns now as the story proper asserts itself. A prison journalist for the *Folsom Reporter* is interviewing the various racial groups on the yard, who are all asserting themselves as No.1, the crew in charge of things. Mann cuts between these groups and therefore highlights the stark racial divisions that exist in Folsom and the justifications each group gives for its perceived dominance. As Mann has noted in his commentary track on the *Heat* DVD, prisons typically exhibit all the normal characteristics of open society – sexuality, gang structures, commerce – except, of course, that they're all hugely ramped up and exaggerated in jail. Here the African-American group promote their vigorous weight-lifting regime, while the Chicano crew stress their primacy in the handball ranks and the white supremacists, run by Dr. D, show their rule over the distribution of contraband. Quite distinct from this is Murphy who now finishes up his run for the day with a final exhausting sprint, the African-Americans, Chicanos and white supremacists a blur of motion as the camera follows Murphy, alone, to the finish line. Yard time is over and the inmates file indoors as the title credits appear onscreen. We glimpse the riflemen in their high towers here, complete with requisite mirrored shades and stark demeanour; *The Jericho Mile* however is not really a prison film that deals with the tension between inmates and the wardens that is so much the focus of other entries in the genre. Its drama is drawn from other sources.

While most of the prisoners now relax with either a rerun of a televised game show or a book from the library cart, Murphy cools down in his cell, trying to recover from his punishing run on the track. For Murphy his running is a form of catharsis and flagellation. He uses his track time to both escape the confines of Folsom and punish himself for the murder of his father. Now in his cell, a space utterly bereft of personal expression or home comforts, he is utterly exhausted and paces back and forth trying to walk away the pain in his legs. Stiles' cell, by comparison, is cluttered with photos and trinkets from his former life; the juxtaposition of mise-en-scene is a little forced by Mann but effective nonetheless – it says what it needs to about Murphy's philosophy. If the mise-en-scene wasn't enough Mann also deploys a shallow depth of field that appears to squash Murphy between the back wall of his cell and the bars that hold him, the metaphor of a caged animal there for all to see. As the higher echelons of prison management begin to take notice of Murphy's athletic ability the film begins to spend some time in the offices of the bosses where unusually avuncular wardens and managers actually work to organise some official running opportunities for Murphy so that his mettle might be professionally tested.

This is not the kind of altruism we have come to expect from prison movies and certainly not in the years 1978-79, when cinema audiences were witnessing the sadism and indifference of the penal system in films like Alan Parker's *Midnight Express* (1978) and Don Siegel's *Escape From Alcatraz* (1979). Both of these films deal with institutions that are so infiltrated by barbarous managers and fiendish wardens

Stiles' cluttered cell

that the only way their central convicts will survive is by busting out, the act of escaping being the source of the expression *midnight express*. That both these films are based upon true events, where the main characters do successfully escape their respective prisons, is perhaps testament to the manner in which the prison system was viewed by movies at this time. Despite repeated viewings we still vie with Clint Eastwood's Frank and Brad Davis' Billy Hayes in their audacious escape bids, such is the power of the negative characterisation of their prisons and those in charge there. Another prison film from the 70s that elevates the notion of escape to near parodic levels is *Breakout*, director Tom Gries' 1975 Charles Bronson vehicle about a wife who enlists the all action star to bust her wrongly convicted husband out of jail. The histrionics of the whole thing may mask the fact that, again like *Midnight Express* and *Escape from Alcatraz*, *Breakout* is actually based on a true story and deploys the same repugnant prison warden characterisations (this time, Mexican wardens and guards as opposed to *Express'* Turkish and *Escape's* American screws) in order to promote the prison break narrative that caps the movie and generate sympathy for the main character.

This feeling, however, is oddly absent from *The Jericho Mile*. You never feel like you want Murphy to escape from Folsom even though his whole raison d'être – running – is completely anathema to the notion of imprisonment and confinement. Prison is where Murphy lives and we, the audience, are just as resigned to this as he is. As Vincent Gaine notes in *Existentialism and Social Engagement in the Films of Michael Mann*: 'Rain Murphy in *The Jericho Mile* understands that running the Olympic Mile will not release him from his life sentence, but he pursues his record breaking time regardless.' The drama of his narrative comes not from his escape attempts (which he could have mounted if he wanted to – one scene shows him being allowed outside the prison walls for an extended run!) or the brutality of the guards or the sadism of the chief warden but from... the prison's desire to see him recognised.

This is perhaps the source of the film's seeming naivety. Audiences presume that prison is an extremely tough environment where violence, extortion, rape and racism are all facts of daily life there. Of course, *The Jericho Mile* explores some of these elements – Stiles' extortion and eventual murder at the behest of Dr. D, the racial divisions and antagonism of the rival crews – but they are all, in the end, transcended by Murphy's record-breaking run and the catharsis of him smashing the stopwatch at film's end. The overall optimism of *Jericho's* construction of both its prison environment and Murphy's character arc – and the positive or negative connotations you take from these – remain, however, a tantalising part of the film's overall appeal and its odd place in Mann's filmography. The simulated realism generated by the film's use of genuine Folsom convicts, authentic Folsom locations and its accrual of West Coast prison culture offsets the naïve optimism of its narrative. Mann was no doubt aware of the tension here and his navigation of the two halves as the story unfolds is at times skilful and not always lacking in subtlety. That being said, so far in the film there is little evidence, visually, that this is what would become known as a *Michael Mann film*. As a motion picture that could bolster Mann's application for auteur status, *Jericho* evinces a flatness in its visual construction that, while perhaps the product of more than one factor, nonetheless renders the piece as anomalous as, say, *The Keep* (1983) in some respects. In particular, the film suffers from that quintessentially 60s/70s lo-fi, blue hue common to

Polaroid photography and related mediums of the period and while this is not necessarily an issue in itself, when combined with working, first and foremost, within the constraints of television, *The Jericho Mile* does not always distinguish itself visually in the way that Mann's subsequent work would. Again, this is not to detract from what strengths *Jericho* does have, merely to suggest that its relevance to Mann's future work lies for the most part in its evocation of prison culture rather than in its technical prowess (an imbalance films like *Heat* and *Public Enemies* would certainly correct).

Following the scenes where the prison management pull strings to get some state sports coaches in to visit Murphy, Stiles gets in deep with Dr. D. Stiles is desperate for a conjugal visit with his wife and approaches one of D's lackeys about organising such a visit; in return Stiles will acquire the extra sugar that D's crew need for their pruno operation to continue, following the isolation of a key former member. Stiles fails to understand the scope of D's operation and the depths of his depravity and becomes subject to extortion in the form of being a drug mule for D's influx of contraband. By virtue of their close proximity to each other in the cells and their shared time on the track, Murphy becomes implicated in Stiles' desperate situation and regards such an intrusion as a violent disruption of his regimen. A key scene exploring this dynamic follows just after the African-American crew has assailed Stiles and Murphy for their involvement with Dr. D. Both men are back in their cells and Murphy is initially haranguing Stiles about allowing himself to become exploited by Dr. D. Mann frames the two cells frontally, allowing for both a visual and thematic opposition to be established between these two men. Stiles, angered by Murphy's indifference to his plight, offers an equally angry but highly insightful analysis of Murphy's shortcomings in a manner, rare for *The Jericho Mile*, that resonates with some of Mann's future work. Thematically, this is the moment when the normally self-assured, highly disciplined protagonist is ably deconstructed by an outside party and, therefore, in the process learns a valuable truth about them self. It's there in the diner scene in *Thief* where Tuesday Weld's character confronts Frank's criminal past; it's there when Lektor dissects Will Graham in the mental institution in *Manhunter*; in *Heat* there are several such moments, the best of which must be the coffee shop meeting of Hanna and McCauley; and *Collateral* (2004) has its moment in the taxicab where Max pierces right to the heart of Vincent's pathology with his 'there are standard parts that are supposed to be there in people and in you... aren't' speech. Visually and thematically, these moments are all of a kind, blocked so as to present the two characters in each instance as binary opposites of one another and written so that what emerges is the acknowledgement of the key character's true self and their real reasons for being involved in crime. As a totem of existential philosophy, The Jericho Mile is, in this aspect, very much in step with a large part of Mann's overall body of work.

Stiles highlights that Murphy is hiding from the truth of his prison existence by denying himself normal pleasures and instead punishing himself with running and isolation. Murphy retorts that he doesn't want his time to be characterised by anything other than running, that he has no need for wives or friends or conjugal visits. As before, Murphy accepts his sentence and doesn't want to dilute the potency of it with the kind of distractions that Stiles invites. And yet the final shot of this sequence has Murphy bowing his head in a kind of mix of realisation – what Stiles has said is very accurate – and sadness; his mystique, the secret to serving out his time, has been exploded by Stiles. In the next scene Murphy is back to punishing himself, albeit witnessed by the state sports coach whom the prison warden has called in to time Murphy's run. With a mile done in 3m 59s the coach is impressed enough to invite Murphy to attend try outs for the upcoming Olympics. Murphy reacts angrily to such an offer, seeing it as an unwarranted distortion of his self-determined regime, and storms back to his cell. At the same time Stiles has learned that the conjugal visit between him and his wife, set up by Dr. D, is nothing but a ruse to get Stiles to ferry drugs into Folsom; the woman who turns up is not his wife but someone from the outside working for Dr. D. Stiles refuses to be party to this extortion and, like Murphy, angrily returns to his cell leaving the woman to be taken into custody by the wardens.

The sequence that precedes the two men arriving back at their cells is the last that Stiles and Murphy will have together. As Stiles, Richard Lawson has a powerful moment here as he laments how prison has stripped him of his dreams and expectations for his life; that, in reality, nothing actually happens here because the individual never seizes the majority of opportunities that come his or her way. This requiem for the acts of self-determination and actualisation bring to mind Vincent's (Tom Cruise) key scene in *Collateral*, Mann's 2004 hitman thriller, where Cruise's character berates taxi driver Max (Jamie Foxx) for never having really pursued his dream of owning a limo company. As Vincent observes of Max's inability to act:

> Someday, someday my dream will come... one night you'll wake up and discover it never happened, it's all turned around on you... didn't happen, never will, cause you were never gonna do it anyway.

Stiles narrates similar ideas here, as he loses himself in a wash of self-pity and fear, made impotent by his inability to navigate the treacherous shoals of the prison system and realise his life with his wife and daughter. But more pointedly these ideas strike at the heart of Murphy who, only moments before, *rejected* the opportunity of running in the Olympics and thus realising his dream. In an attempt to purge himself of this feeling Murphy insists that Stiles must try to get himself into solitary confinement or onto a transfer as quickly as he can, these being the only methods of avoiding the violent retribution that is surely heading his way from Dr. D. Stiles agrees to meet Murphy on the other side of the dining area and, from there, form a plan to avoid Dr. D's wrath. It is here that *Jericho* generates its first sense of real danger as Mann delineates the way in which violence comes for you in prison – abruptly and without the possibility of escape. Murphy is locked in his cell by a goon posing with a library cart and, despite hollering and shouting, cannot get Stiles' attention as he makes his way to the meeting point. Mann preludes the murder to come with several cuts to the tattooed abdomen of Steve White, the real convict mentioned earlier, who sports a swastika and 'white power' design tattooed on his stomach and wielding a shank behind his back. Stiles enters a sort of caged antechamber where the doors are shut and he is stabbed to death by White, the photos of his wife and new daughter clutched tightly in his hand as he slumps forward and down against the wire fencing. Murphy overcomes the makeshift lock on his cell door but arrives too late to save Stiles.

(left) A real convict; (right) Murphy's spartan cell

Mann's direction off this pivotal scene in the film is surprisingly restrained and perhaps even a touch moribund for those of us more accustomed to the rigorous sense of pathos that would normally accompany such a moment. There is a sentimentality to the death of Stiles that, while perfectly justified by the events that have preceded it (and seeming almost in harmony with the film's developing naivety), concurrently seems at odds with *Jericho*'s strive for realism, a realism that was so fervently pursued in the opening minutes. The musical cue Mann brings in as Murphy rocks back and forward in his foetal position of guilt and rage is shamelessly effective. It demarks his point of no return, the jumping off spot from which Murphy will now at least recognise the idea of the prison as a collective environment that can be experienced. Stiles' death forces Murphy to make this change in his philosophy and thereby honour his only companion in Folsom by acknowledging that they did in fact have a friendship. The choice of Jimmie Haskell's music here makes this awareness of Murphy's character unavoidable but also brings to light the real skill that Mann will soon wield in his musical accompaniments and cues. He would soon become known for true avant garde selections, be it his fondness for Lisa Gerrard and Pieter Bourke's ethereal New Age soundscapes, or for making new use of established artists such as Tangerine Dream and Moby. Through his now practiced use of these artists, music in general has become such an integral, intricate, irreducible and *subtle* part of Mann's visual storytelling that Haskell's melodramatic choice of music for the death of Stiles in *The Jericho Mile* seems quite obtuse and even gratuitous by comparison. It tugs at the heartstrings a little too vigorously and renders what should have been a moment of poignancy into something bathetic and jarring.

From here Murphy realigns his priorities and informs the prison that he *will* run for the Olympics but with a few conditions of his own. Murphy asks to be allowed into the 'metal industries' room alone in order to 'do something for Stiles'. Murphy gives the warden the kind of *here and now* ultimatum favoured by a number of other characters in Mann's canon; *decide right now, yes or no because there is no time to wait, to ponder and then make your choice*. The warden agrees and Mann's camera tracks Murphy left to right as he then strides through the metal industries room, Mann even using a fast zoom (to remind us that this is the 1970s!). Some of Dr. D's cronies are told to clear the room and Murphy is then left alone, the prison officer wandering off oblivious to what's about to happen. *Jericho*'s view of prison culture reveals its native naivety again here as Murphy is left alone to smash up the workshop in a slo-mo paroxysm of what initially looks like blind rage but becomes about something else. Murphy checks the back of each smashed tool cabinet before moving on to the next and eventually locates his quarry, the very meat of Dr. D's *metier*, his ill-gotten drug money. Murphy's on the yard now with the drug money in one hand, a can for burning it in the other. From behind the wire fence that surrounds his perch on the prison bleachers Dr. D, with just a hint of irony, asks 'He's gonna burn something, what's he gonna burn?' Murphy immolates the dollar bills as Dr. D realises the fire's fuel and yells that he's 'looking at a dead man'. Mann cuts to a long shot of the pyre and then to a close up, the burning heap becoming a kind of prison Olympic torch for the running events to come.

Murphy's now outside the walls of Folsom, doing a series of practice runs with his spikes on in a scene that represents the height of the film's naivety and optimism in the nature of prison culture. His new mentor hands Murphy a stopwatch, *the* stopwatch, with the inscription *To the Jericho Mile* on the back. He runs off down the track followed by his mentor in a slowly moving car, the quarried walls of Folsom to screen right and the desolate winds of change blowing on the soundtrack. From here Mann segues into the bureaucratic preparations of the Chief Warden, as he tries to navigate the bureaucratic nightmare of giving a prison inmate the chance to run in the Olympics. In order to allow Murphy to qualify the warden agrees to build a quarter mile track in the yard. The labour for this eventually comes from a willing racial cross-section of the prison population – a kind of penological *if you build build it they will come* for Folsom – the sweep from which will keep Dr. D and his murderous intentions from reaching Murphy for the moment. A scene follows that tries to articulate and justify the naivety of *Jericho*'s view of prison life and Folsom's elevation of Murphy to near poster boy status. The Chief Warden says:

> This thing happening could mean more to convicts all over this country than 15 years of rehab programmes put together... Murphy's the model for connecting to the outside. Backing him means a lot. Cause not connecting means staying into those games on the yard, then they hit the streets and cop out into their comic book fantasies, screw up an armed robbery, kill a few people and then they're right back in here.

There is a great deal of sense and affirmative thinking here. However it is this kind of pro-active imprisonment, this rehabilitative methodology for the treatment of criminals, which quickly becomes conspicuous by its absence in Mann's later crime films. Consider again Dennis Haysbert's character Breedan in *Heat*; he gets paroled out of jail and takes a job working as a grill man for Bud Cort's restaurant manager. But instead of being permitted the chance to re-enter society and work for a living, Breedan is extorted by the corrupt manager, who tells Breedan that 25 per cent of his wages goes back to him or he will bust Breedan back to jail on a phoney charge. *Heat*, like *Thief* before it or *Public Enemies* after, shows a great degree of cynicism towards the prison system of the West Coast and the Mid-West respectively. *Heat* deconstructs the rehabilitation programmes of Folsom and Chino – similar to the one Murphy is now pioneering in *The Jericho Mile* – and presents instead an alternate (but perhaps more truthful?) reality of how prisoners are received on the outside, *if* they actually make it to their release date.

Despite the prison's appeals to the inmate population to help build an Olympic grade running track on the yard, the project falters as Dr. D forms a political picket line ostensibly in protest at such a proposed exploitation of prisoner labour. D's real motivations for the picket line are, of course, maintaining the racial supremacy of his white supremacist gang and exacting revenge on Murphy for the burning of his drug money. This

Dramatic overhead shot, a la *Taxi Driver*

kind of bleak virulence blunts the edges of the film's earlier optimism and returns *The Jericho Mile* – albeit briefly – to a kind of realism, the realism that audiences *normally* ascribe to cinematic views of prison life: self-interest, hostility, violence, isolation and hopelessness. This mode continues as Dr. D suggests (falsely) to Cotton (Roger E. Mosley's character) that it was Murphy's involvement with Stiles that eventually led to the latter's murder. Cotton directs Murphy to the laundry area and proceeds to beat him up in a protracted sequence that wears its metaphorical significance a little to obviously on its sleeve. Beaten but not broken, Murphy is then helped to his feet by Cotton, a gesture of both solidarity (by the end of the beating Cotton seems to acknowledge that Murphy had nothing to do with Stiles' death) and patronisation (at this point Cotton is still bound to the notion of the racial hierarchy on the yard). It is the next scene, however, that offers up a cathartic turning point in the development of Cotton's character and the film's view of the ethos of Folsom Prison. Having purged himself of his racially-inflected paranoia via his ceremonial beating of Murphy, Cotton approaches the Chicano convicts on the yard – a moment set beneath that same mural of Death that opened the film – in an attempt to cement an opposition to Dr. D's picket of the track building project. The Chicanos agree to join Cotton's militia and the new, larger group now assail Dr. D's supremacist barricade in a violent melee of shivs, shanks, bats and bars. This riot sequence is one of the few instances in *The Jericho Mile* where a genuine feeling of threat and danger is communicated to the audience. Six convicts are hospitalised by multiple stab wounds but the point is made to Dr. D: the racetrack *will* be built and Murphy will have his climactic run. Before the riot scene ends Mann surveys the carnage by cutting to an overhead shot of the discarded weapons and injured men in a manner redolent of Scorsese's famed overhead shot of Travis's carnage towards the end of *Taxi Driver* (1975). Although not used to suggest a mental dislocation or disassociation in the way that Scorsese intended, this overhead survey is still meant to invoke a similar feeling of disgust and, more importantly, closure or withdrawal for the audience – Mann, like Scorsese, is saying *be reassured, the 'bad bit' of the film is over and we can now proceed with the uplifting part*.

In the qualifying race for the Olympics Murphy beats the other 3 contestants and runs a mile in 3m 52s. Mann ably captures the unifying force of the race on the usually fragmented prison population. The diegetic sounds of the crowds chanting and cheering and yelling recall the whoops and cries of the Huron war party in Mann's 1992 film *Last of the Mohicans*, while his use of slow motion as Murphy breaks through the finishing line tape is shamelessly effective at crystallising the triumphalism and melodrama that lies at the heart of the film. Murphy's validation is, however, short lived as Mann interjects events with the banal reality of normal life that often plagues his characters, something Neil McCauley would refer to in *Heat* as 'barbeques and ball games'. Murphy is denied a place in the Olympics due to him being an inmate who shows little signs of having been 'rehabilitated', in the words of the Olympic board member. Dr. Bill Janowski (Geoffrey Lewis) replies that such a term 'is no longer current', pointing towards an understanding that Folsom Prison, at least as it exists within the confines of the film, should be viewed not as an institution bent on 'correcting' Murphy but instead providing him with opportunity worthy of his latent talent. This kind of notion again alludes to the sense of naivety coursing through *The Jericho Mile*, a sense that is by now obviously being *intentionally* cultivated by Mann. In this sense, *The Jericho Mile* may have more in common *tonally* with Frank Darabont's redemptive *The Shawshank Redemption* (1994) than it does with other prison films of the 1970s or '80s.

The climactic sequence of *The Jericho Mile* provides the viewer with a welcome reprieve from what one might term the dour optimism of its narrative up to this point. Having been forced to accept the Olympic board's decision, Murphy returns to his state of penal acceptance, of serving out his sentence in accordance with his self-imposed dictum. As the momentum of the Olympic bid begins to fade, the old racial structures and divisions reassert themselves as the heightened reality of prison life comes, once again, into play. The African-Americans resume lifting weights, the Chicano convicts return to their handball and Dr. D's white supremacist crew are back peddling drugs and creating a false sense of purpose on the bleachers. There's something oddly reassuring about this given the chaos and upset to the established order that Murphy's Olympic bid seemed to cause. But Murphy is hurting. When all hope of a true atonement for him seems lost, Mann reintroduces that strange little convict character from the opening minutes of the film – the radical and revolutionary inmate with a hi fi who's still bopping to the sounds of his music – and thus posits the idea that something good may still happen.

This little cameo character serves a very similar narrative function as the man with the green radio does in Mann's 2001 epic *Ali*, the muscular biopic about the irreverent boxer's decade long journey to the Rumble in the Jungle. In that film the man with the green radio also appears twice during the film's running time. The first instance is when Ali is running through the backstreet slums of Kinshasa and witnesses the man among the crowds that have gathered next to the hand drawn murals of Ali smashing the tsetse flies and tanks; the second is when, nearly beaten by George Foreman during the climactic Rumble bout, Ali looks to the crowd, once again spots the man with the radio and is imbued with an invincible spirit that allows him to win the fight. The reappearance of the convict with the hi fi in *The Jericho Mile* is most certainly an analogue or precursor to this idea. He's back again, invoking the radical spirit of the '70s and the insurrectionary idealism that, like in *Ali*, says an individual *can* speak truth to power and win against the established order. Murphy's out on the track once more, aware that the Olympic race is taking place very soon but equally aware of the need to return to his old life. Mann cuts to the man with the hi fi, who seems to be jiving to both music and the radio commentary emanating from the Olympic pre-event, such is the playful nature of Mann's diegetic sound design. The commentator proclaims 'Frank Davies blew everybody away with a time of 3m 50.6s in the mile... and is the number one miler in the States', the sound overlapping several cuts to other prisoners and finally ending up at Murphy's cell. Mann reminds us of the extent of Murphy's entrapment in Folsom by cutting to this shot of him in his cell, one that's very similar in its composition to an earlier shot where Murphy was buttressed and barricaded by the walls and bars of his fate. Murphy is viewed here much in the same way as he was subsequent to Stiles' murder, both events – his friend's killing and his ejection from the Olympic bid – serving as catalysts for inner change. Murphy is blocked between the bars of the cell door, back to the audience and head down in a posture of solemnity like some reversed version of Aaron Shikler's famous portrait of JFK. Imbued with the desire to prove his worth he grabs his running shoes and heads to the yard track for one last time, the moment demarked by a return to the Stones' 'Sympathy for the Devil' on the soundtrack.

(left) The hi fi man returns; (right) discarding the watch

Murphy runs his mile and beats Davies' time. The prison unites around him and Mann captures Murphy's victory in another splurge of glorious slo mo, the runner crossing the finish line with arms outstretched in a gesture that seems to say, 'I did it, now do with me what you will'. Murphy knows he's beaten Davies' time but the other prisoners rally around him to check the numbers. Murphy then launches his stopwatch high into the azure sky, eventually causing it to smash against the perimeter wall into several pieces. There is an obvious aspect to the symbolism here that perhaps masks the underlying ambiguity of Murphy's climactic actions; does he smash the stopwatch because he's achieved the ultimate validation in his life and is happy to discard it or because the stopwatch has been the source of a deviation from his rigid doctrine of self-flagellation for the murder of his father? Does he return to the track at the end to prove to himself that he is the best or to atone for his inability to prevent the murder of Stiles? Is it enough that the only recognition Murphy will get for his winning time is from Folsom itself and not the outside world? There is both a positive and negative connotation to the action of smashing the watch that renders these questions at once troubling and fascinating in the pursuit of a closed reading of The Jericho Mile.

There is, then, much to admire in The Jericho Mile. It is a film of some quality, no doubt, and certainly fights above its weight in terms of narrative ambition and its pursuit of verisimilitude, particularly in its deployment of real Folsom locations. The film's view of prison culture is interesting and useful in a limited way when we consider the importance of this theme in some of Mann's future work. It presents some of the character archetypes and traits that will later feed into the figures of Frank in Thief, Neil in Heat and Dillinger in Public Enemies and is notable for its use of real Folsom convicts in some of the key roles. The Jericho Mile is nevertheless a minor work (did it demark a sonorous arrival for Mann in the way that something like Who's That Knocking At My Door? (1967) did for Martin Scorsese?) when factored into any assessment of Mann's auteur status. From this perspective it can be concluded that the film is not an indispensable progenitor of Mann's related future work – in the way that his next film would be – due to its paucity of two things: an overt technical presence (on the part of Mann) and those wonderful narrative opportunities from which emerge the pathos and sense of modern, existential alienation that now characterises his best efforts. In some ways The Jericho Mile is like Steven Spielberg's Duel (1971) in that both were highly impressive made-for-TV debuts that nevertheless bear few of the hallmarks that would later characterise both directors in later life. With Duel there is a cynicism and flat linearity to its tale of an everyman pursued by the murderous truck that, slight elements of Jaws aside, would quickly wane as Spielberg's more veritable traits and tropes began to gain traction. With The Jericho Mile, instead of Duel's cynicism, there is a melodramatic naivety to its view of prison culture and the opportunities given to Murphy that seems at considerable odds with what would soon constitute a large part of Mann's MO; namely his much more morally neutral to negative view of the penal system and its ability to 'rehabilitate'. It is interesting to consider then that the cynicism that so aptly characterises Duel would soon become Mann's typical view in some of his key films, whereas the naive optimism of The Jericho Mile would quickly pass to Spielberg and colour much of his work, at least until Schindler's List (1993).

So *The Jericho Mile* is a valiant attempt at perhaps opening up the form of prison dramas endemic to the 1970s. It is also the source of one or two enduring Mann narrative traits when looked at from the perspective of 2013. And yet, it must remain a marginal work when folded into our assessment of Michael Mann as an *auteur*. Using Andrew Sarris' criteria as a guiding principle for this, while the film is *technically competent*, it is not in possession of a demonstrable or *distinguishable personality* and certainly seems devoid of an obvious *interior meaning* that could be thought of as common or unique to Mann. For this writer it must be thought of as an interesting curiosity with some tenuous links to what would follow.

From top: Warden Norton discovers Andy's secret, The Shawshank Redemp-tion; *Ed Norton,* American History X; *Free at last – Tim Robbins in* The Shawshank Redemption

Prison and Punishment, Race and Redemption:

Comparing Prison Life in *The Shawshank Redemption* and *American History X*

by Peter Turner

Introduction

The most beloved film of the 1990s and furthermore the number one film on the Internet Movie Database's Top 250 film list is about prison and redemption. It features a central pair, one white American and one African American, one innocent (perhaps) and one guilty and it deals with how hope and determination can change their lives. It is, of course, Frank Darabont's *The Shawshank Redemption* (1994), adapted from a Stephen King novella. But there is another film of the 1990s that warrants investigation and comparison to this most popular of fables, when considering race and redemption in prison films. While *American History X* (1998) is not strictly defined as a 'prison film', the entire narrative pivots on the central prison scenes and the redemption of the main character, from racist bigot to redeemed and reformed ex-con, is all down to his formative time in prison.

Sean O'Sullivan has already pointed to the similarities and fundamental differences between these two opposing films arguing that '*American History X* is in some ways almost a mirror image of, or answer-film to, *The Shawshank Redemption*' (2001: 322), an idea that will taken forward and expanded on in this article.

The prison film has a long and varied cinematic history with narratives and themes of escape, brutality, hope, despair and redemption all being consistently revived with new incarnations and incarcerations. The 1990s had a range of prison set films from the comedic (*Ernest Goes to Jail*, 1990) to the deadly serious (*Dead Man Walking*, 1995) but none tackled redemption and tied it in to representations of race in such interesting ways as did *The Shawshank Redemption* and *American History X*. These two films also represent prison in time periods decades apart. Michael Fiddler argues 'the prison came to project (or we project upon the prison) the sense that it was a repository of dark, unconscious fears' (2007: 193). He suggests that the gothic nature of older representations of prisons made them appear fearful as opposed to more modern representations of prisons as a part of urban landscapes. This is interesting to note in the differences between how the Shawshank State Penitentiary and the California Institute for Men are represented in the films. O'Sullivan (ibid: 321) believes that the 'imagery and its connotations needs to be considered if we are to understand the cultural significance of representations of prison in film'.

There are many reasons to look at these two films and many ways to explore how they construct their representations of race and redemption. Racism and racial divisions will be considered as the films differ greatly in their portrayal of these ideas. The suggestion of prison as a place for punishment or for redemption will also be explored. Despite the fact that prisons are segregated by gender and the characters are all male, the issue of race and gender will also need some consideration. The last century saw an exponential growth in numbers of people incarcerated and many 'opponents of prison growth have begun to investigate the role of the mass media in fuelling growth of the prison population' (O'Sullivan, 2001: 317). Through looking at the representations of race and how redemption is achieved in the films, it is the intention of this article to reposition *American History X* as actually a more progressive text than its more popular and palatable 'mirror image'.

Racism

Black and white mingle freely in *The Shawshank Redemption*

Racism is a key theme of *American History X* whereas it is an issue that is largely ignored in *The Shawshank Redemption*. Though much of the narrative of *American History X* takes place outside of the prison, racism exists within the walls as clearly as it exists outside; on the beaches, basketball courts and in the high schools of Venice Beach. O'Sullivan (2001: 328) calls its representation of LA and its prisons a '"city of division"... ruled by "ethnically" self-segregating gangs'. Though *The Shawshank Redemption* is set between 1949 and 1966, a time when racism was no doubt rife in America and when outside Shawshank's walls the civil rights movement would have been in full swing, racism is never witnessed within the prison, not from the guards or the inmates. In fact Shawshank is a prison where African-Americans are clearly the minority and blacks and whites mix seemingly in perfect harmony. Despite Morgan Freeman's voiceover intoning that 'prison is no fairy-tale world', O'Sullivan (ibid: 327) argues '*The Shawshank Redemption* imagines a fairy-tale world in which racism is virtually absent. *American History X* seeks to put white racism on display in full view'. Freeman's character, Red, is the victim of no racial hatred and could easily be seen as the leader of the group that become Andy Dufrense's (Tim Robbins) friends. The otherwise white group respect Red and treat him as an equal, if not their intellectual superior. There is no hint of racial tension between the inmates whereas the prison in *American History X*, though appearing in the present day and supposedly a more liberal and tolerant age, positively seethes with racial strains.

Perhaps the reason for the lack of racism within Shawshank's prison walls is that in the source for the screenplay, King's novella 'Rita Hayworth and Shawshank Redemption', the character Red is 'so called because he is a red-headed Irishman' (Fiddler, 2007: 197). Therefore if the source lacks racism due to Red's character not even being African American, then the adaptation is unlikely to force this theme into its story despite the casting of Morgan Freeman. Also if we take the reasons that Danny (Edward Furlong) in *American History X* gives for becoming part of a racist skinhead gang, then we can see that there is less of a reason for the inmates to hate Red. Danny argues that Derek (Edward Norton) formed the DOC (Disciples of Christ) because white kids were scared of black gangs and were tired of being pushed around. Racism in this context comes out of a fear of black youths and particularly groups of black men that intimidate white men. An early scene in *American History X* shows this exact scenario where a young white man is being bullied, pushed around, sworn at and beaten by three black youths in a high school toilet room. However in *The Shawshank Redemption*, the prison is mostly filled with white men and the African-Americans are clearly far in the minority. Perhaps this could be seen as a reason for the lack of racism as the white inmates have no reason to fear the blacks as they are few and far between in a film that 'produces a predominantly white main cast and only a weakly multi-racial *mise-en-scene*' (O'Sullivan, 2001: 326).

Whether this ethnic diversity is an accurate depiction of an American prison in the 1950s and '60s is worth investigating. Black people are notoriously over represented in real-life American prisons as well as movie representations and, though the state of Maine where the film is set 'ranks just behind Vermont as the whitest state in the nation' (Long, 2012), Shawshank is still a prison that is oddly lacking in much racial diversity. Perhaps this is a refreshing change from the stereotypical black criminals of so many other representations of prison or perhaps it is all part of the 'fairytale' that *The Shawshank Redemption* creates. Fiddler (2007: 203) argues the film 'cannibalizes existing images and meanings of the prison to produce its own wilful nostalgia' and 'not only tolerates, but also thrives on, a misrecognition of the past it evokes'. The film does indeed produce nostalgia and posits a past where whites and blacks were equal and live in racial harmony. Race is never mentioned, black characters are treated no differently by either inmates or guards and Red is respected amongst his peers. Unlike the prison in *American History X* there are no racial divisions or tension between characters of different races.

On the other hand the later film takes a completely opposite stance to race relations. The prison appears segregated along racial lines. The scenes in the exercise yard feature groups of white skinheads sitting around staring at the blacks, Latinos and other ethnicities. There is no mixing except when one of the characters (Mitch) is seen dealing with a Latino. In *The Shawshank Redemption*, Red describes himself as a character that can get a man anything from the outside world. *American History X* also shows a prison where a non-white character is needed to get contraband. In this case the audience assumes it is drugs and Mitch is using his contacts outside the skinheads to deal drugs to other white prisoners. It is interesting to note that in both films ethnic minorities are seen as the people that can get illegal goods from the outside, as if criminality is a profession or a compulsion and something that cannot be stopped merely by putting these characters in prison. Whereas in *American History X*, Derek finds the dealing of drugs from non-whites to whites despicable, the characters in *The Shawshank Redemption* find Red's ability to acquire goods acceptable, useful and even a means of bonding. It is also interesting to note that in the scene in The Shawshank Redemption where the chain that goods go through to get to Red is laid bare, many of the inmates involved are black, again highlighting the criminality of these characters.

One way in which the films differ considerably is in their focus on the black characters. While *American History X* may have many more black characters in the *mise-en-scene*, they are almost completely ignored in terms of their perspective, back stories and character development. *The Shawshank Redemption* includes only a single black character of note but the story is his story, Morgan Freeman's narration giving Red's perspective on Andy's long journey from new inmate to escapee. The only similar character in *American History X* is Dr Sweeney (Avery Brooks), the principal of Derek and Danny's high school and the visitor to Derek when he is at his lowest in prison. Dr Sweeney is comparable to Red in that he is a wise, mature black man who offers advice and cares for a younger white character but *American History X* is not his story. In *The Shawshank Redemption* the relationship between Andy and Red is one of relative equality with Red mentoring Andy to begin with but Red also learning a lot from Andy as time passes. In fact, Andy is very much seen as a civilising influence on his fellow inmates including Red. He gets Red a job as his assistant, offers to teach him chess and opens all the inmates' ears to the wonders of operatic music. It is a typical representation of the educated white man that can offer culture and refinement to those 'beneath' him. O'Sullivan (2001: 327) argues that through 'the casting of Morgan Freeman as co-lead, the film is given an appearance of racial equality which it in fact does not live up to'. Theorists have noted in the buddy cop action films of the 80s such as *48 Hours* (1982) and *Lethal Weapon* (1987) the idea of having black and white co-leads often meant that the black lead is dominated by the white character. *The Shawshank Redemption* conforms to this notion with its 'buddies' Andy and Red; Andy being the innocent unjustly imprisoned (he claims) and Red the convicted and guilty murderer ('the only guilty man in Shawshank') who learns from his more civilised, educated and respectable buddy. Ed Guerrero (1993: 239) argued 'Hollywood has put what is left of the Black presence on the screen in the protective custody... of a White lead... and therefore in conformity with dominant, White sensibilities and expectations of what Blacks should be like' with Donald Bogle (2001: 272) later offering 'interracial buddies can be such only when the white buddy is in charge'. Morgan Freeman's Red, like the black buddy cops before him, is made safer to a white audience as this murderer is surrounded by whites, 'civilised' by Andy and stripped of any African identity.

On the other hand Dr Sweeney and Derek begin with a strained relationship but are never on equal ground; Sweeney is always in control; the wise mentor. It is Derek's respect for his teacher that attracts the ire of his father when he becomes interested in the black literature Dr Sweeney encourages Derek to read. But when Derek is savagely raped in prison by his fellow skinheads, it is Dr Sweeney that arrives to comfort him, bring him books and offer him a new path in life. Though we learn little of Dr Sweeney, he reveals that he too had a troubled past and that hate blinded him as a youth and caused him to seek to blame those around him for the bad things in his life. Therefore it is not completely true that, as O'Sullivan (2001, p.328) suggests, 'the black characters... have no history and the story is not told from their perspective'. Dr Sweeney is mentor and teacher to Derek, the civilising influence to Derek's brutal savage. The other black character that *American History X* introduces and offers some insight into is Lamont (Guy Torry). Again this is a character that Derek comes into contact with in prison when he is forced to do laundry with him. Lamont is a stereotypical black youth; loud, obnoxious and funny but he is also caring and considerate. He soon becomes Derek's saviour in more ways than one. Lamont allows Derek to see the injustice that black people can suffer at the hands of a racist legal system and also breaks down barriers by bonding with Derek over basketball and sex. It has been argued that 'the black male is unable to conceive of the female as like or necessary and can acknowledge her only through domination' (Jones, 1993: 252) and *American History X* partly perpetuates this with Lamont's descriptions of relationships and 'make-up sex' that are crude and allow the two men to find common ground in their amusement at women.

American History X has been criticised by some for limiting the representation of racism to individuals and skinhead gangs rather than focusing on institutional racism. However Lamont's story about how he ended up in jail for assault rather than burglary does hint at the prejudice he likely faced from the police force. It has also drawn criticism for its representation of Derek before he is sent to prison as 'it has been suggested that the film... implicitly valorises his behaviour' (O'Sullivan, ibid.). The scenes of his brutality towards the gang members who attempt to steal his car do risk glorifying the notion of a strong and fearless white man, bulked up like a Nazi super man and ready to tackle the criminal elements of black society. O'Sullivan (ibid.) even goes so far as to claim that 'despite its intention to challenge racism, the film succeeds only in reproducing it'. With poor representations of black youth that perpetuate stereotypes it is understandable but the character of Dr Sweeney is the most sympathetic, righteous and heroic of all the characters in the film and goes some way to challenging the idea that *American History X* reproduces racism. Despite the racial divisions represented, the time devoted to Derek's extreme politics and the fact that it is a black youth that shoots Danny at the end of the film, the message is one of tolerance and redemption; a call for both races to rise above a perpetual cycle of hatred.

Punishment

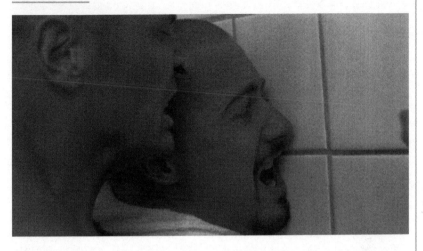

Punishment, *American History X* style

In *The Shawshank Redemption* and *American History X*, however, the prisons are not simply sites for redemption but, in line with what society expects of real-life prisons, also places of retribution and punishment. Much is made in today's media of modern prison life being too 'easy' or too 'soft' on prisoners but both of these films show a very different representation of US prison life over the last half century or so. Punishment can come in many forms and have many effects on the prisoners. The question of what prisons are used for and why we have such institutions is the subject of numerous books and this article is not the place for that discussion. However both films pose interesting ideas about how punishment is inflicted on prisoners, by whom and to what ends. O'Sullivan (2001: 318) considers the issue of 'the influence of representations of prison in mainstream popular film on people's perception of the legitimacy of imprisonment as a form of punishment' in his article. With *The Shawshank Redemption* one of the most popular films of all time according to some sources, is it fair to assume that its representation of prison affects audience perspectives on real-life prison?

In *The Shawshank Redemption* the prisoners all insist on their innocence, except for Red who admits his guilt. However rarely do we learn anything of the crimes the prisoners committed in order to be convicted and imprisoned. Similarly, in *American History X*, viewers only learn about Derek's crimes and what his new black friend Lamont did to end up incarcerated. Red and Lamont both admit their guilt but Lamont insinuates that he was the victim of a racist police force that argued he was committing assault rather than merely burglary. Red is rejected for parole time and time again throughout the film, perhaps in some part due to his race though this is never stated. O'Sullivan (2001: 321) argues 'the message of prison movies is implicitly that prisoners deserve what they get' though this is not true of Lamont and one wonders if many viewers consider the need for Red to remain incarcerated essential. Without knowing more details about his crime it is hard to say whether he deserves to spend more of his time in prison, although he seems harmless for the duration of the plot.

The notion of prisoners 'getting what they deserve' is further undermined in *The Shawshank Redemption* with Andy's repeated stints in solitary confinement and his sexual abuse at the hands of other inmates. Rather, the message of *The Shawshank Redemption* is that an innocent man can maintain his self-respect through nineteen years of perseverance, hardship, determination and hope no matter what challenges and obstacles he faces. The Shawshank Redemption takes a sympathetic look at elderly prisoner Brooks also, suggesting that his long life in prison has made him so institutionalised that he is terrified of the outside world. His suicide is possibly the biggest tragedy of the film, despite Brooks being a convicted murderer. Brooks' punishment it seems never ends with Red arguing when they give you 'life' that is exactly what they take.

Much of the punishment dished out in the films comes from figures of authority. Derek is abused on his first day behind bars by a Latino guard, making him even more nervous about his precarious position in prison. Another guard turns a blind eye when Derek is being attacked by his fellow inmates. These acts help to make prison appear as an unwelcoming, brutal place where punishment is meted out to the guilty. In *The Shawshank Redemption* the authorities are more major characters and are variously represented as corrupt, vicious and sadistic but there is also some complexity in how the audience is invited to read their actions. For example Warden Norton (Bob Gunton) and Captain Hadley (Clancy Brown) are essentially positioned as the villains of the film. Warden Norton might be a man who firmly believes in the teachings of the Bible but he is also corrupt; accepting bribes and having a prisoner shot for revealing a truth that could damage his position. He is sadistic, taking great pleasure in locking Andy up for daring to try to prove his innocence. Even more so is Captain Hadley who puts a new prisoner in the infirmary for crying at night and is a brutal bully. However, in line with the idea of prisoners getting what they deserve, Captain Hadley and his men also savagely beat one of the prisoners (known as the 'sisters') who have been raping and assaulting Andy. This moment in the film relishes the fact that Bogs is now crippled and can no longer be a threat to Andy. So while most 'prison authorities are either unable or unwilling to protect the lives and wellbeing of their charges' (O'Sullivan, 2001: 328), Captain Hadley briefly does become a 'hero' of the film in saving Andy from further abuse at the hands of other inmates.

Prison is a place full of dangerous individuals and although the actions of other inmates are obviously not officially sanctioned forms of punishment, it is easy to see part of prison life's hardships as the consequence of being incarcerated in a place full of violence and savagery. Tuszynski (2006: 120) argues 'it has become commonplace for a prison movie to address the idea of sexual threat within the prison system'. Rape appears to be one of the most hideous, degrading and savage forms of punishment that prison has to offer. Though the authorities have little to do with it, there could be more done to stop the actions of inmates toward each other. The guard that shuts the door, allowing a gang of skinheads to rape Derek is acknowledging and therefore unofficially sanctioning the assault. Similarly, Andy is continuously targeted by the 'sisters' and nothing is done about it until they put Andy in the infirmary and Andy has helped Captain

Hadley out with his tax returns. Only then is something done to stop the abuse. Therefore as O'Sullivan (2001: 326) suggests, both films are 'characterised by high levels of institutionalised inmate violence' that become a form of unofficial punishment part and parcel of incarceration itself.

It is also interesting to consider how much these instances of punishment are represented as catalysts for redemption. Andy's first two years in Shawshank are defined by his fights with 'the sisters'. His steely determination to break out of the confines of the prison could be conceived as coming from his desperation to escape this most savage and extreme form of punishment in his early days of incarceration. More immediate, however, is Derek's turn from racist thug to reformed model prisoner in *American History X*. After he turns against his own skinhead gang, he begins developing a relationship with Lamont. Instead of glaring silently as Lamont attempts to engage him in conversation, Derek begins to converse with him, first over women and then over basketball. It is when Derek starts playing basketball with the black inmates that his old friends brutally rape him in the shower. Lamont foreshadows this scene when he tells Derek that 'in the joint, you the nigger not me' and when the rapist attacks Derek he says 'you wanna be a nigger, we gonna treat you like one'. Derek is punished for his own perceived racial transgressions having turned against the skinheads for their own dealings with other ethnicities.

Derek's rape is certainly the catalyst for his change and eventual redemption. He is visited in the infirmary by Dr Sweeney who brings him books and offers him sympathy. Derek rejects the skinheads completely after he recovers and thanks to Lamont and Dr Sweeney, he makes it through prison without further harm and with the promise of setting his brother Danny straight when he gets out. If Derek's punishment beyond merely being incarcerated is being raped, then it is indeed an *effective* punishment, and this is where a morally complex film perhaps becomes confused. Are we to interpret the abuse suffered by Derek as somehow being 'good for him', an extreme form of 'whatever doesn't kill you makes you stronger' philosophy? Or is it an unequivocal evil from which good emerges?

Redemption

Derek, Andy and Red all find some sort of redemption in *American History X* and *The Shawshank Redemption*. In both films the bond between a white man and a black man aids these characters in finding their own forms of salvation. King & Leonard (2004: 42) argue 'the idea of redemption through friendship and integration infects a spectrum of films'. Andy and Red help each other through their prison terms, and Lamont certainly helps Derek through his. What the films do not do, as O'Sullivan (2001: 321) notes, is 'show the inmate population as a whole of being capable of collective redemption/rehabilitation'. Brooks fails spectacularly to be reformed, first putting a knife to a fellow inmate's neck when he first learns of his impending release and then committing suicide when he feels incapable of reintegrating into a world that has moved on without him. Red eventually manages to convince the parole board that he is ready for release by

Lamont (Guy Torry) is the agent of Derek's (Ed Norton) redemption

showing regret but dismissing the concept of rehabilitation. Andy is described by Red as a bird too bright to be caged and escapes, finding his own liberation through determination, perseverance and cleverness. Derek is surrounded by gangs of blacks and whites that appear to have only grown harder, angrier and more intimidating during their time in prison. It is only he who finds redemption through a combination of white brutality and black kindness.

In this sense, *The Shawshank Redemption* and *American History X* differ in their representations of race and redemption. *The Shawshank Redemption* mostly conforms to traditional representations of the relationship between black and white characters. Red learns from the more cultured and clever Andy, whereas in *American History X*, it is the black characters that 'teach' Derek. King & Leonard (ibid.) argue: 'filmmakers repeatedly tell stories of interracial friendships resulting in the redemption or growth of the white protagonists. Whereas in the past, films presented the maturation of black characters through their contact with whites, recently, a role reversal has taken place within Hollywood.' Red learns to hope, to appreciate opera and to use his time productively in prison under the tutelage of Andy. Though Andy is a beneficiary of Red's ability to get anything into the prison (particularly the rock hammer and posters) and receives some sound advice from Red early in his incarceration, it is mostly Andy who offers Red a chance at redemption. Even the climax of the film allows the pair a happy reunion on a beach in Mexico thanks to Andy's cunning planning and generosity to his old friend. A slightly different perspective on this is suggested by Nero (2004: 46) who argues 'a white male, who appears to have a marginal status in society, but in actuality has an enormous capital of high culture, teaches a man of colour about opera… The tutored character is transformed toward a greater humanity'. So it can be argued that there is a two-way relationship in that Andy gains something from teaching Red about opera but this is less clear than the retribution offered to white characters through their contact with black characters in *American History X*.

American History X completely reverses these traditional roles. Derek is 'a white character, limited by his own flaws' who 'grows merely by knowing a "black buddy," who serves as the catalyst for change and eventual redemption' (King & Leonard, ibid.). Derek's racism makes him angry, aggressive and lands him in prison. Dr Sweeney offers sympathy when he is at his lowest and also brings books to ensure Derek continues his education. The reason he visits is through concern for Derek's brother, Danny. Dr Sweeney is therefore responsible for both brothers' possible redemptions. Similarly Lamont offers Derek a new way of looking at black people as they find common ground and Lamont tirelessly tries to engage Derek. Lamont might arguably be a more stereotypical representation of black men, with his criminal past and 'street talk', but he is a good soul and it is thanks to his connections that Derek is not targeted by black inmates after he falls out with the skinheads.

Conclusion

The Shawhank Redemption and *American History X* offer very different representations of prison life (although there are also some similarities in the representation of prison). *The Shawshank Redemption* negates what audiences know about race relations in America of the 1950s and '60s and offers a simplistic and nostalgic look at a prison undivided along racial lines. It is also more conservative with its white hero arriving in prison and teaching the inmates, including black inmate Red much about hope, 'civilised' behaviour and arts. It paints a picture of corrupt officials prone to bribery and savagery but then valorises the behaviour of one guard when he cripples an inmate in a savage attack.

On the other hand *American History X* offers perhaps a more realistic (and, consequently, grim) look at life inside a modern prison. Completely segregated into gangs of whites, blacks and Latinos, the prison of the 1990s is a site of continuing racial hatred. In opposition to Shawshank's mixing of races and Red's complete acceptance into a group of white inmates, Derek enters a prison where he must choose a side in order to be protected from other gangs. The swastika tattoo on his chest unsurprisingly initially positions him in opposition to non-whites and helps him to easily fit in with a group of white skinheads; but it is this same group, that initially seems to offer salvation, that actually is his greatest threat. *American History X*'s Derek might be like *Shawshank*'s Andy in that he is white, smart and well-educated but Derek is also blinded by anger and propaganda and requires the sympathy, understanding and compassion of black characters to help him find redemption.

Prison films offer audiences a peek inside a place many of us will never visit. These two films show the problems that media representations often focus on, such as inmate violence, corrupt guards and the issue of whether prisons are really for punishment and retribution or truly for rehabilitation. *The Shawshank Redemption* mostly depicts inmates who cannot be rehabilitated or cannot survive in the outside world due to institutionalisation, whereas *American History X* suggests that rehabilitation can stem from unlikely sources – both the savagery and compassion of fellow inmates and persistence of supportive individuals on the outside. Through hope and perseverance, Andy manages to escape. Derek's struggle will begin when he is released, though the final scene of the film suggests that his final punishment is greater than anything prison can offer.

Bibliography

Bogle, D. (2001). *'Toms, Coons, Mullatoes, Mammies and Bucks: An Interpretive History of Blacks'* in American Films. New York: Continuum.

Fiddler, M. (2007). 'Projecting the prison: the depiction of the uncanny in *The Shawshank Redemption*' in *Crime, Media, Culture* 3 (2), pp.192-206.

Guerrero, E. (1993). 'The black image in protective custody: Hollywood's biracial buddy films of the eighties' in Diawara, M. (ed.) *Black American Cinema*. London: Routledge.

Jones, J. (1993). 'The Construction of Black Sexuality' in Diawara, M. (ed.) *Black American Cinema*. London: Routledge.

King, C. & Leonard, D. (2004). 'Is Neo white? Reading race, watching the trilogy', in Doty, W. (ed.) *Jacking in to the Matrix franchise: cultural reception and interpretation*. New York: The Continuum International Publishing Group Inc.

Long, 2012 http://bangordailynews.com/2012/09/14/politics/understanding-why-maine-is-so-white/

O'Sullivan, S. (2001). 'Representations of prison in nineties Hollywood cinema: from Con Air to *The Shawshank Redemption*' in *The Howard Journal* 40 (4), pp.317-334.

Nero, C. (2004). .Diva Traffic and Male Bonding in Film: Teaching Opera, Learning Gender, Race, and Nation' in *Camera Obscura* 19 (2), pp.46-73.

Tuszynski, S. (2006). 'A cold war cautionary tale: heterosexuality and ideology in William Wyler's *Ben-Hur*' in *Journal of Popular Film & Television* 34 (3) pp.116-122.

OUT NOW

Studying Fight Club

Mark Ramey

" ...a convincing argument for the ongoing relevance of [Fight Club's] themes and ideas... extremely well-written and considered... crammed with a full range of accessible and varied theoretical frameworks... "

Media Education Association

auteur

Top down: Tom Hardy as 'Britain's most dangerous prisoner', Charles Bronson

Infamy, Masculinity and Violence:

Bronson and the cult of Celebrity

By Will Rimmer

Introduction

My name is Charles Bronson, and all my life I have wanted to be famous...

The opening line (told in self deprecating voiceover narration) to Danish director Nicolas Winding Refn's 2009 Brit flick *Bronson* summarily epitomises the parallel contradictions of the films titular protagonist cum anti-hero. The second part of the line is certainly true, as the film which this article attempts to decode evidences the unyielding Bronson obsession with fame and celebrity. He craved the spotlight in such a way that every Andy Warhol stereotype is undoubtedly fulfilled (that is, the Warhol proclamation that everyone in their lifetime will be famous for at least 15 minutes). Moreover, another fair assumption would be to suggest that Bronson achieved fame in a manner even he, with his wild imagination, could never have envisaged. Yet would the word 'notorious', rather than 'famous', be a more accurate perception of a man who has spent well over 37 years (including a staggering 31 years and counting in solitary confinement) - pretty much his whole adult life - living at Her Majesty's pleasure?

In fact, even the statement '*My name is Charles Bronson*' hides a basic truth, and the film's thematic subtext regularly delves into the complexity of what is truth, and what is mere fantastical exaggeration. The infamous British prisoner Charles Bronson, dubbed by the press in general terms as 'Britain's most violent convict', was born under the real name of Michael Gordon Petersen, on 6 December 1952, in the mid-Wales town of Aberystwyth. It may be surprising (or not, depending on your opinion of the man) to ask why it took such a long time for biopic to be made about such a well known British figure? It may also be surprising to learn that when the film did finally get the green light to go into production, it was made by a quirky foreign director (the aforementioned Dane Winding Refn) on a modest budget, with marketing capital kept to a minimum by distribution company Vertigo films.

The expectation in film circles was for the project to be made by an established home grown British film-maker, who would undoubtedly had more prior knowledge of the subject in question. Yet even though Refn was not familiar with the back story of such a larger than life figure, he understood what it is that makes Bronson tick, and found a way to illustrate the many paradoxes within his life onscreen. The resultant film does not suffer due to being made by an essentially art house, indie director like Refn.

It could be argued that a more neutral, objectively colder eye that an émigré filmmaker brings to the table balances out the dangerous potential for glorification and deification that a British director may have fallen foul of, intentionally or otherwise. All of this, of course, is mere conjecture and speculation, as Bronson is resolutely a Nicolas Winding Refn film, and further viewings serve to cement both his auteur status, (and in this writer's view, at least) the film itself as an underrated modern classic.

Nicolas Winding Refn: the wild child

The director, who hails from Copenhagen, starting making films at an early age, which ensured the Danish press dubbed him in his early days as L'Enfant Sauvage (the wild child). Prior to Refn, Denmark had recently produced film-makers as divergent as the controversial Lars Von Trier, whose films routinely shock and enthral viewers in equal measures across the world. Other prominent luminaries of Refn to emerge from Danish cinema in the 1990s include Thomas Vinterberg, whose impressive debut film, *Festen* (1998) was created out of the short lived *Dogme '95* style of film-making which was started up primarily by himself and Von Trier as a reaction to the artificiality of commercial mainstream (Hollywood) cinema.

Dogme '95 promoted a back to basics method of film-making, known as the 'Vow of Chastity', with all technical tricks (e.g. post-production sound effects, elaborate lighting systems, camera tracks, props, etc.) and other such techniques bein eschewed in favour of 'true' realism and naturalised methods. Though such an approach could have easily failed, it did initially work to an extent, thanks to a strong storylines and committed actors. Von Trier followed the Vow of Chastity approach himself with a particularly controversial film from his back catalogue, *The Idiots* (1998); and although *Dome '95* as a formal doctrine was shortly abandoned, it's influence arguably lives on insofar as it acted as some sort of model for independent film-making.

Though Refn didn't fully participate in the *Dogme* movement, the stylistic influences have resonated in his work, most notably in the *Pusher* trilogy of films. The first was released in 1996, and is a violent, unflinching portrayal of life in Copenhagen. The Pusher films became something of an indie cult phenomenon, and helped boost Refn's profile, both at home and abroad, as a director willing to take risks, and be iconoclastic in nature. *Pusher 2* (2004) and *Pusher 3* (2005) sealed this reputation, leading to *Bronson*; after which he made *Valhalla Rising* (2010), a story about a Norse warrior named One Eye, who is powerfully played by Mads Mikkelson – who, neatly bringing the recent history of Danish cinema full circle, recently starred in *The Hunt* (2012), directed by *Dogme 95* founder Vinterberg.

In film-making terms, Refn has often cited Martin Scorsese as a huge source of inspiration. Certainly, In *Bronson*, Refn deploys two typical Scorsesian touches effectively, that of subjective narration, and inspired use of extra-diegetic music. The eclectic mix classical music throughout the narrativ, serves as a soothing antidote to the on screen anarchy we see Bronson act out. The projects Refn has chosen throughout his career have regularly caught people by surprise, and there is no reason to presume that will change.

Speaking in an interview for the *Bronson* DVD special features, Refn discussed how he wanted to find different layers of storytelling, to convey how Bronson could be perceived as a performer struggling to find a loving audience appreciative of his creative talents:

He wants to be an artist. Find his stage. How can I reinvent this man as a showman? He is a great publicist. I was thinking a lot about American independent films in the 1950s and '60s. Here, it was very fragmented storytelling, it was almost experimental to its approach. You mix different layers of storytelling. There is the real world [at home with his parents]. There is the world that Charlie wants us to see him in [e.g. the animated scene towards the end]. There is the Charlie deep down who kind of narrates [opening scene after the prologue]. Then there is the Charlie on stage. That really is what he is looking for. He is an artist looking for his stage. *Bronson* is really an allegory, a metaphor for becoming an artist; and finding a way to work within that, and then wanting to be famous... that is why I came up with the line at the start of the movie, which basically starts the whole thing off.

'The Man. The Myth. The Celebrity.'

On the promotional posters for the film's (short) theatrical release, the words 'man', 'myth' and 'celebrity' are used to help sell it to the public. Over the years, many journalists have tried with varying degrees of success to get underneath the skin of Charles Bronson, and try to work out who he is in reality, and understand the motivations for a lifetime pattern of self destructive behaviour which many a prison psychiatrist and psychologist have been unable to fully comprehend. Spending his adult life in prison (apart from a couple of briefs periods of freedom totalling 69 days since his first armed robbery in 1969), with solitary confinement the extra punishment for a catalogue of violent misdemeanours, the irony has not been lost on observers and social commentators that 'Britain's most violent prisoner' has not, incredibly, killed anybody in his entire life. Not during periods of freedom, or during the ongoing stretch of incarceration. He has not committed the sorts of heinous crimes that are unspeakable, yet still find the perpetrators released back into the wider community after receiving a 'life' sentence. While such criminals have benefited from the inconsistencies of the justice system, Charles Bronson, it seems, will rightly or wrongly spend the rest of his natural life in prison. His last parole appeal in 2009 inevitably failed, as the British Government have no intention of releasing him now, or in the future. For Bronson, life really does mean life.

Bronson supporters believe he has been left to rot in prison, yet despite this seemingly unjust treatment of him, compared to other prisoners released, it must be noted Bronson did commit violent acts to other prisoners, wardens, and ancillary staff such as teachers. It is hard to imagine they will ever recover from his reign of terror either physically or emotionally. As a pivotal scene in the film illustrates, the 1999 kidnapping of prison teacher Phil Danielson in Hull jail highlighted just how dangerous a man he is, when the mood swings fluctuate so arbitrarily. The Hull incident is one of many jail sieges, hostage situations, prison warden attacks, rooftop demonstrations and countless threats to harm others which have seen Bronson moved a staggering 121 times from one prison to the next. He has been sent to all three of England's maximum security hospitals: Broadmoor, Rampton secure hospital and Ashworth hospital.

Alongside the human cost of his antics, the financial cost to the taxpayer of his rooftop demonstrations is estimated at well into the millions. As an example of Bronson's warped state of mind, in 1998 he took Iraqi hijackers and another inmate hostage at Belmarsh prison in London. He demanded they call him as 'General' and told negotiators he would eat one of his victims unless his demands were met. Later, he demanded a plane to take him to Cuba, with plenty of ammunition, and an axe. In court, Bronson confessed he was 'As guilty as Adolf Hitler...I was on a mission of madness, but now I am on a mission of peace, and all I want to do is go home and have a pint with my son'. Another seven years were soon added to his sentence.

As newspaper headlines continually describe Bronson as both man and myth, it is difficult to ascertain reality from fiction. He has not been shy to self promote his achievements over the years, as despite being inside, Bronson has successfully published books and exhibited artwork in galleries commanding over £2,500 a canvas. Despite having turned in December 2012, Bronson insists he can still get through 2,500 push ups a day; thus maintaining muscular physique men half his age would struggle to achieve. As we see in the film, the sheer brawn and overpowering physicality of the man requires several wardens to stop him, and only then with great difficulty!

Narrative Structure in *Bronson*

For storytelling purposes, Refn uses a fragmented, non-linear method of narration, but in such a way as not to confuse the spectator. We flip between different decades, as Refn charts the key events which shape the ultimate direction of Bronson's life. After the opening prologue, the initial scenes illustrate the early years, from infancy to delinquent schooldays, to the frustrations of working in a fish and chip shop. Voiceover narration offers Bronson's thoughts on his early years.

The 1950s, when he is born, are highlighted, with the infant Bronson amusingly shown in a wooden cot; the bars the young tot grabs with his hands clearly standing in as visual metaphor for the prison cell bars he will become more familiar with in years to come. The 1960s scenes see Bronson cause havoc at school. Bronson is shown terrorising one of his teachers, and picking up a desk ready to throw it at him. Indeed, the scene indicates how Bronson's problems with institutionalised authority figures and organisations started at a very early age. The 1970s are covered through the brief relationship he had with his first wife, Irene (they married in December 1970) – Bronson was just 18 years-old – and then the fateful Post Office armed robbery incident in Ellesmere Port, Cheshire, which landed him with a seven year stretch. Only £26.18 was stolen in the botched job, but Bronson's fate was sealed. The 1980s section of the film detail not just the prison/mental hospital life we know about (which will be discussed later on), but also the 69 days of freedom he tasted, and his struggles to cope on the outside. Liberty comes at a price for Bronson, the ultimate example of institutionalised humanity. The outside world now is his cage, rather than the prison walls.

Illegal bare knuckle fighting scenes present Bronson as a man who only knows the language of violence, as a means of making quick and easy money. By the end of the film, the 1990s are mainly documented with the 1999 hostage scene of teacher Phil Danielson at Hull Prison. Recent years are not covered, and Refn is less concerned with the specific name-checking of places and time periods; instead what we get is a character study, rather than a direct biography which has a neat narrative chronology. Such are the contradictions of Bronson's life, it is perhaps appropriate for Refn to play fast and loose with events. Refn's version, after all, is loosely based on significant events in his life, and does not purport to provide an objective 'truth'. The film, as Refn has been at pains to point out, is intended as an entertainment piece, not a documentary. His story is about Charles Bronson the performer, and not the 'madman' of the British tabloids.

Subjective voiceover narration is a clever device used early on to help the spectator identify directly with Bronson. We are now with him every step of the way in the story – whether we like it or not. The relationship has been formed, and there is no turning back. Anchored against the montage of shots for each decade previously described, his voice emits a tone of weary resignation as he begins:

> Right, how else can I explain it? There was nothing wonky about my upbringing. My parents were decent, upstanding and respectable members of society. I went to school, kept my head down. Sort of like most kids, I got into trouble. I liked it. But I wasn't 'bad' bad. And I still had my principles. I took the first job I could get my hands on. I suppose the crumpet wasn't bad...
> 1974. A tough time to be young in England. Not a lot of opportunity around. Still, life moves on. Irene and I got hitched. It was alright. We didn't have it bad for a couple from the chippy. But they don't give you a star on the walk of fame for 'not bad', do they? So this is the Post Office I did over, this is what I got away with [£26.18], and this is what they gave me [seven years].

The voiceover link harks back to the voiceover of Alex De Large in Stanley Kubrick's *A Clockwork Orange* (1971). Here, another vicious anti-hero made cut from the same cloth as Bronson himself, tries to garner empathy with the spectator, by regularly describing himself as 'Your humble narrator'. It is almost as if he is describing someone else entirely, as if the terrible crimes we see Alex commit (vicious assault, rape) were not his fault. The difference with Bronson's narration, however, is that he has a semblance of self-awareness. He cannot talk about himself in the third person. He knows, even though he may ask the audience to feel sorry for him, it is a losing battle. Bronson has also been compared to the Eric Bana character Mark Read in the film *Chopper* (2000), written and directed by New Zealander Andrew Dominik. It is not hard to see the parallels between the two men. Both are 'lifers' who used self-promotion and notoriety to acquire a cult following. A compare and contrast analysis of both films may garner interesting results for any film student of the prison film sub-genre.

Britain's next big star?

The actor who took on the role of Bronson, Tom Hardy, was enthusiastically praised as the next big thing for his stunning *tour de force* breakthrough performance. His star has been rising at an exceptional rate, and in February 2011, Hardy won the prestigious Orange 'Rising Star' Award at the BAFTAs. With Bronson, Hardy effectively 'did a De Niro', by taking a transformational role where he has to physically change his body to match the real person he is playing. Robert De Niro famously won the Best Actor Oscar for his portrayal of 1950s boxer Jake La Motta in *Raging Bull* (1980), directed by Martin Scorsese.

Just as De Niro underwent a punishing regime to add the required muscle to his slim frame, Hardy hit the gym obsessively to transform his body (with particular emphasis on the upper body, triceps and biceps) to replicate the look of Bronson. In total, 3 stone of pure of muscle was added and, in true Method Actor mode, Hardy aimed to equal the rumoured regime of 2,500 press ups a day achieved by Bronson himself. Other actors in recent years to go down the transformation route include Daniel Day Lewis' Oscar winning portrayal of Cerebral Palsy victim Christie Brown in *My Left Foot* (1989), and, perhaps the current king of character immersion roles, Christian Bale, who bulked up impressively for films like Mary Harron's *American Psycho* (2000) where he played psychopathic 1980s Wall Street yuppie Patrick Bateman, and the Bruce Wayne character in Christopher Nolan's reboot *Batman Begins* (2005). Prior to *Batman Begins*, Bale alternatively endured dramatic weight loss, this time to play haunted insomniac Trevor Reznik in *The Machinist* (2004). He dropped down to just 8 stone 9 pounds, which sparked fears about the health of the actor, as he looked quite skeletal onscreen. In March 2011, Bale won the Best Supporting Actor Oscar, for his performance as boxing trainer Dickie Eklund, in *The Fighter* (2010). Once again Bale dropped several stone in weight, though not to quite such emaciated levels as in *The Machinist*.

Another link between both Bale and Tom Hardy is the Batman sequel, *The Dark Knight Rises* (2012). Bale returned as Bruce Wayne/Batman, opposite Hardy in the role of arch villain Bane. One factor which helped Hardy snag the role, surely, was his last film was the Christopher Nolan head scratcher *Inception* (2010). Ironically, Nolan himself had not even seen *Bronson*, the film which many critics and fans in the online community pre-supposed was the main reason Hardy was offered the role (it transpired that Nolan was intrigued by Hardy's small role as Handsome Bob in the Guy Ritchie crime drama *Rocknrolla* [2008]). For Hardy, a stealthily sharp rise up the Hollywood ladder to the A list, follows on from young British talent such as Keira Knightley, Orlando Bloom, Robert Pattison, Andrew Garfield, Daniel Radcliffe and Carey Mulligan storming the gates. It will be interesting to see if, in future years, Hardy continues to choose small character driven pieces, in the vein of Bronson, or follow the mainstream blockbuster route a la the Batman film.

'The Loonie Bin': Bronson v Broadmoor scene analysis

Twenty minutes into *Bronson* there is a scene which typifies how the film's tone can switch seamlessly from the serious to the surreal, as Bronson is confined to an institution (Broadmoor). Bronson's refusal to conform to prison norms over the years leads to hospitalisation. Descriptions such as the 'funny farm' are inevitable. In the previous scene he has again refused to accept medication from prison wardens, leading to another predictable beating. The audience is not explicitly told the name of the institution Bronson has been sent to, or even in what year the scene takes place. The spectator must work this out, and, anyway, this is not too important. The scene exemplifies the nadir to which his existence has now dropped.

The mental hospital/asylum has cinematic comparisons to the Oscar-winning film *One Flew Over the Cuckoo's Nest* (Milos Forman 1976). Seeing Bronson amongst such disparate characters indicates just how bizarre a situation he has now got himself into. It is possible to feel empathy for Bronson, thrown in with such pathetic looking characters.

Rest and recreation in Broadmoor

The first shot is a slow left to right tracking shot following a man walking from one end of a room to another. Diegetic muzak plays in the background. The man is framed in a profile long shot as he walks, and we see a fairly unusual bunch of people in the background. Some patients are playing catch together, others are simply sitting down. Some are walking around aimlessly, another playing tennis shots to an imaginary opponent. Two patients walk around what appears to be a medical screen, incongruously out of place in what appears to be a large ballroom or sports hall. The exact milieu is something of a mystery, as the look of the room is as arbitrary and conflicted as the personalities who inhabit it. As the slow tracking shot continues, we see a small gaggle of patients sitting quietly watching television, quickly followed by a shot of a man rocking back and forth at a table and chair. He appears isolated; alone and vulnerable. Harsh overhead lighting accentuates the effect that these people are trapped, but trapped within the confines of their own troubled mental states, rather than the more obvious physical confinement. Finally the camera stops, and then begins a reverse journey from right to left of the screen where it settles on Bronson, who we see sitting spaced out on a chair, drugged up to the eyeballs. It is both an image both funny and disturbing. The unnamed walking man approaches Bronson, and quietly speaks to him:

> Thing is, they don't understand. They will never understand. And that scares them. So they keep you drugged up. What is that going to change? It ain't gonna change the you inside. I think I know the truth. You're no more mad than I am. Yes, it's all just made up. It's rubbish...

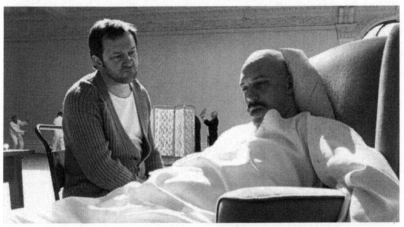

'You're no more mad than I am...'

The man seems friendly enough, yet in subsequent conversation with Bronson, he reveals himself to be a paedophile, something Bronson finds abhorrent. The following medium close-up shot of Bronson shows him frothing at the mouth. He can't stand. He can't talk. He sits in a trance-like state. It is almost as if he has been lobotomised. The earlier Charlie we knew, the cheeky full of life anti-hero of before, has been replaced by a robotic mannequin, devoid of feelings, emotions or any human resonance.

An editing dissolve turns into a wide angle, bird's-eye view shot of the whole room. Refn's camera peers down to the survey the scene. In the foreground is empty space; off to the right, we have two hospital wardens standing guard, ensuring nothing dangerous or subversive takes place. In the background, the motley assortment of patients can be seen dancing together. The music playing is the Pet Shop Boys' 'It's a Sin'. The diegetic music suggests the scene taking place could be around 1987, when the song was originally released. The deployment of the song riffs on the idea that Bronson believes that what the establishment are doing to him is as much a sin as any that he has committed. It is an absurd scene, yet funny nonetheless.

Out of the group emerges Bronson, dancing with an anonymous woman. He is wearing white overalls with a dark cardigan. He wears a tie, yet without a shirt

and collar. His slippers further accentuate the randomness of his clothing. A slow forward tracking shot, in point of view perspective, visualises how Bronson wants to escape from the room. It looks as though only Bronson of the room's inhabitants can truly understand the absurdity of the events taking place around him. He has to escape, and quickly.

The main door is blocked by a metal barrier, which again revisits the film's central visual motif of cages/entrapment. (The final shot of the film will see Bronson, appropriately enough, locked up in his cage; a grotesque animal on display for the amusement of his prison guards.) He walks towards the blocked door like a zombie, or even the monster from *Frankenstein* (1931) instead.

A reverse tracking shot follows, as Bronson now moves with a greater sense of urgency towards the door. Escape is just yards away. Again from his viewpoint, we see two guards in plain white uniform move menacingly towards our protagonist. Without the need for words, Bronson is pointed back in the direction of the dancing patients. Any escape bid is futile. A wide angle shot frames Bronson alone in the centre of the room; in a relatively long take, devoid of cuts, he walks over to the central seating area. The bird's-eye view from the start of the scene is repeated, followed by a dramatic shot from above Bronson's head. He starts to scream and cry, his sense of frustration and anger rising to a crescendo of internal and external exasperation. The music equally rises to match his sense of injustice and institutionalised straight-jacketing. He shouts out the 'C' word which ends the scene (the liberal use of such strong language throughout the entire film is a prominent aural motif). When it comes to articulations of the English language, Bronson is clearly no wordsmith. He speaks as he acts; unapologetically, without any sense of remorse, totally in-keeping with his natural instincts. The following scene begins with a voiceover from Bronson, back in semi-confessional mode and talking direct to camera against a black background, which further accentuates the bleakness of his current predicament:

No way out

Fucking loonies they're great, mate, but, well, they are fucking loonies aren't they? I had to get out somehow. This was not a hotel I wanted to stay at anymore. Being a celebrity and all I needed to check out. And I had a good idea how to do it...

In the scene that follows, Bronson attempts to strangle the friendly paedophile. He is restrained by the guards and dragged away, face smiling, ready for another beating but out of the hospital.

Social and political contexts

Both the violence and the swearing in the film, it could be argued, are less provocative than cathartic in their purpose. Certainly, the liberal use of the dreaded 'C word' mouthed consistently by Bronson, serves to shine a light on the more appalling behavioural traits he simply cannot change within his physical and psychological make-up. On the film's surface, Bronson may well be a horrific creature, someone regular people could not try and begin to understand. Social anthropology studies may well consider mankind, and its variant customs, in all its forms. Yet men like Bronson can easily fall outside of what most people – even Bronson's fellow prisoners – deem 'normal' behaviour. But after all, in an increasingly dysfunctional and fractured era of social disintegration, what is 'normal'?

Deluded or not, the Bronson we see in the film is a man who considers himself exempt from the parameters of acceptable social behaviour. Just as many of the great male loners in the Westerns of John Ford (usually played by John Wayne) worked to help people in society, they paradoxically struggled to live within that same society themselves. These ironies are apparent to the audience, if not the characters onscreen. For Bronson, he sees himself as a man willing to challenge and take on the system, whatever the personal cost to him. Others will benefit from his acts of violence and roof top protests. Though this is hard to fathom, and Refn offers no easy solutions either, the audience are given enough encouragement to feel that Bronson is hard done by, both by the state, and by the media, who lapped up all the crazy antics he had to offer.

He may come across as half man, half animal, but the reality of Bronson as a product of his social environment, lacking in opportunity, and thus hope, suggests he should only take some of the blame. The interconnection between individual fallibility and social ills where moral decay breaks down the barriers of acceptable human behaviour is something to be given greater consideration. As a young father and husband in 1974, desperation drives Bronson to rob the Post Office.

The criminal act of the robbery is underpinned by the fact that life in Britain during this time was a tough time for young people, something Bronson is quick to point out for the audience. Should the Ted Heath-led Conservative government of the early 197's be blamed for Peterson's (he hadn't yet taken his 'fighting' name) act of folly? If there are no jobs, what should a man do? Is there any alternative choice? For an uneducated man like Michael Peterson, there was not, and the consequences took hold with alarming speed. The social and economic barren wasteland of 1970s Britain was a far cry from the 'Swinging Sixties' generation, just a few short years earlier. The three day week and energy crisis simply added to the gloom many working class people felt at this time. While the '60s baby boomers indulged in a move towards freedom and excess, promiscuity and liberalism, the austerity of 1970s Britain acted as a precursor to the end game that would reach its final, depressing point of no return during the social, economic and political anarchy that was Thatcher's Britain of the early- to mid-1980s. Furthermore, 1981 was the poster boy year for social and economic deprivation. Not that an incarcerated Michael Peterson would ever get the chance to participate in street riots like those that occurred in Brixton and Liverpool in the summer of 1981. While a Royal wedding took place in July, the streets of inner city Britain burned both literally and metaphorically.

The 1974 Post Office robbery, though only given a short amount of screen time, clearly represented the low point of his life to date. The viewer is challenged with questions about the nature of criminality, and the forces at work to dictate such a desperate act. Does Bronson commit the robbery as a basic necessity to provide for his young wife Irene and their child? Is it simply to put food on the table? Or is there a deeper rooted explanation, which delves deeper into the psyche of a man who sees madness as an equal to genius? Thankfully, Refn does not appear to invite automatic sympathy for Bronson, and other such criminals. Neither does he simplistically seek to blame society. His camera is more of a cold observer of events than an intimate friend of Bronson; this despite the apparent confessional scenes, and performance-related theatre scenes which illustrate Bronson as the ultimate performer – a wannabe vaudevillian hiding behind the skin and face of somebody else. Things are never quite as they seem in *Bronson*, and such ambiguities are precisely where much of the viewing pleasure can be derived. We have learnt that Bronson doesn't ask for, or expect, any kind of empathy from the public. Not even the spectators in his private stage show warm to the man, regardless of the laughs and cheers we hear from them. It is all illusory; fantasy masquerading as skewed reality.

The Charles Bronson we see in the film is a male protagonist typical of being the product of his social environment, and then warped by the allure of celebrity status. But is this strictly true? Over the years, everyone has had their say about the 'real' Bronson, from psychologists to psychiatrists, biographers to so-called celebrities themselves. The most well known prisoner in recent British history got what he wanted, fame in all its contradictory glory and infamy. Yet, conversely, he is a complete enigma. Myth or man? Where does Petersen the human being begin, and Bronson the showman end? Refn's film keeps his true identity frustratingly out of reach. We think we know him, yet we know nothing at all? The vaudevillian stage performer looks real enough, yet is he a mere doppelganger for the man beneath the make-up? The film starts off by dealing with notions of contradiction, and the ending of the film, equally, finds us questioning what is real, and what is fantasy. This perfectly sums up the arbitrary nature of the both the character and the overall film Refn cleverly constructed. Randomness has never been depicted with such clinical precision.

A tough sell?

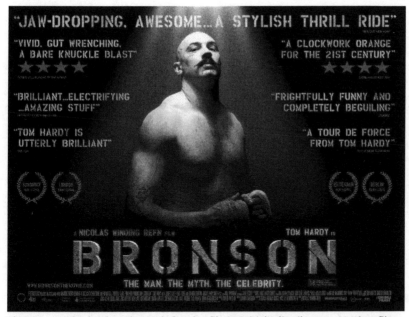

Selling
Bronson

There is no doubt that the task for the film's British distributors, Vertigo films, to get Bronson out there in the market place, and find an audience, would be difficult, if not impossible. An 18-rated prison sub-genre biopic film, with violence, nudity and crude of use of language ensured Bronson would be little more than a niche film in an over-crowded market place.

Previous Vertigo films releases have included British movies such as *The Football Factory* (2004) *The Business* (2005) and *The Firm* (2009), all directed by Nick Love; club culture comedy *Its' All Gone Pete Tong* (2004), gritty crime drama *London to Brighton* (2006), geezer misogynist horror *Doghouse* (2009) and *Street Dance 3D* (2010). The latter film would go on to be something of a surprise sleeper hit, a home-grown crowd pleaser in a marketing dominated by such blockbusters as *Toy Story 3*, *Inception* and *Harry Potter and the Deathly Hallows: Part One* (all 2010).

Bronson was released in the United States on 9 October 2009 opening on just a solitary screen. The three day weekend take amounted to just $10,940. It expanded to a maximum eight screens, during a 73 day theatrical run which garnered a total US box office take of $103,828. Despite such low numbers, the film did find an audience in other territories, resulting in a global theatrical take of $2,260,712 (box office mojo.com). To put this into some kind of perspective, *Inception*, Tom Hardy's first foray in the Hollywood mainstream, went out on 3,792 screens in North America, and reached a worldwide take of $832,584,416. As these figures prove, low budget British films like *Bronson*, however well made, will never match up to the distribution might of the Hollywood studios.

Though *Bronson* was never going to be a box office champion, the critical community did give it generally positive reviews, with particular praise in the direction of star Hardy. Trade paper Variety said:
> Bronson is beautiful. D.P. Larry Smith does stellar work – and Hardy's performance is outstanding, especially considering he's playing multiple parts: There's the war-painted, hell raising Bronson who dives lustily into herds of prison 'screws' and nearly beats them down. There's the briefly out of prison Bronson who, deprived of his natural habitat, becomes meek, vulnerable and, for a moment, the awkward lover of the faithless Alison (Juliet Oldfield). It's not just that he can't function. He is almost invisible. When Bronson reunites with his uncle Jack (Hugo Ross) who runs a brothel/salon for cross dressers, the film starts to flag, because you realize at that point there'd been no story... The director doesn't explain Bronson so much as use him as a mirror for viewers who would probably like to act against the frustrations of life by putting someone's head through a wall.

A review by Robert Hanks, for The Independent suggested:
> Bronson is *The Shawshank Redemption's* dark twin, a film in which the hero, a brute himself, never had any hope or dignity to begin with, is guilty as hell, despises culture, and far from winning freedom just coils himself tighter and tighter into the system. It is also not a realistic picture, despite being to all intents and purposes true... Bronson is an opera or a fantasy, a series of tableaux couched about with elaborate rhetorical devices – Charlie Bronson himself standing erect and pop-eyed, Victorian strongman's moustache bristling like quills on an averagely fretful porpentine, as he spouts his side of the story to the camera... The film doesn't want to treat Bronson as an existential hero struggling to retain his identity in a dehumanising system, but it keeps drifting in that direction. It's not a masterpiece by any stretch; but it's original and pacy, and those qualities are rare enough.

When it came to blogs, and responses to online reviews, generally populated by unpaid critics and non-professional writers, the reactions were more mixed. Many people were angry the film appeared to eulogise a violent prisoner in such a way, while others found the film too arty and pretentious. Another obvious criticism was how the film 'glorified' violence in general, something Refn argued was never his intention. The implicit suggestion here leans towards the copycat theory of audience response. Would portraying Bronson as a role model for anti-social behaviour fuel potential abhorrent behaviour?

Summary

The reasons why *Bronson* makes for such an exciting, visceral cinematic experience are partly down to the talents of the director, and the onscreen star, Tom Hardy. Yet the film also works, because it functions both as a cautionary tale and also as a light-hearted fantasy film – however crazy that might sound having read this article. The generic category may be a 'biographical drama', yet there are enough shifts in tone and mood to take the audience well outside the sphere of depressing kitchen sink realism, a direction in which the narrative could so easily have drifted into had it been in the hands of a different director.

No, *Bronson* works because despite Bronson's appalling character traits, and subversive psychological drives, we still care about him enough to want him to win through, to somehow beat the system; even when we know the odds are overwhelmingly against our protagonist. Bronson may not be liked, he may not be loved, but he can never be ignored, and that, evidently, is where the film succeeds.

References

Websites
www.imdb.com
www.independent.co.uk/arts-entertainment/films/reviews/bronson
www.the-numbers.com
www.boxofficemojo.com
www.wikipedia.org/wiki/Charles_Bronson_(prisoner)

Newspapers

'Bronson's Monster Mansion "Escape Bid"', Daily Mirror 6 December 2010

Film

Interview with Nicolas Winding Refn, *Bronson* DVD special features
Tom Hardy – building the body, ibid.

Resources Reviews

Book review
By John Atkinson

Nosferatu (1922), the vampire ur-text

Ken Gelder, *New Vampire Cinema*, BFI/Palgrave Macmillan, ISBN: 978-1-84457-440-7, £16.99, 2012.
Jeffrey Weinstock, *The Vampire Film: Undead Cinema*, Wallflower/Columbia University Press, ISBN: 978-0-231-16201-2, £14.00, 2012.

'Vampires,' as Anne Billson tells us in her excellent Devil's Advocates monograph (2011) on *Let the Right One In* (2007), 'have never been so popular.' If this is certainly the case today in the cinema, it is also true of critical writing *about* cinema. Barely a month goes by without the publication of an academic tome promising a 'new reading' about some aspect of the comings and goings of the undead, verging dangerously into self-reflexive territory – that is, studies that reflect on the study of the films as much as the films themselves.

In *The Vampire Film: Undead Cinema*, Jeffrey Weinstock attempts the difficult trick of providing a primer for study while at the same time proposing some original ideas. It's written for Wallflower/CUP's 'Short Cuts' series, which is self-described as 'a comprehensive list of introductory texts'. 'Comprehensive' it certainly is, as Weinstock's contribution is the forty-eighth in the series, but I know from reading others that they can't all be considered 'introductory texts'. Some certainly fit this bill, and they tend to be the genre focused titles, but others are much more idiosyncratic and, one suspects, ended up being not quite the book the publisher thought they were commissioning.

But Weinstock scores fairly highly, in part, and perhaps counter-intuitively, by focusing on a relatively small number of films with which to illustrate his arguments (in one instance too small a number, but we'll come to that). He opens by proposing seven governing principles 'that offer some coherence to the category [of vampire films] and go a long way toward making sense of this movie monster's remarkable fecundity' (p.6). These vary from the now fairly commonly understood – 'The cinematic vampire is always about sex' – to the apparently contradictory – 'The vampire film genre does not exist' – and by the end of his introduction Weinstock has done a good job of setting out some ground rules for how to spot a vampire film as well as establishing the spade work for the rest of the book, which is divided into three chapters: 'Vampire Sex', 'Vampire Technology' and 'Vampire Otherness'.

A selection of well-chosen case studies illustrate the author's discussion, notably the *Blade* series (1998–2004), which pops up throughout the text, most notably in the 'Vampire Otherness' chapter, which is largely about race. Weinstock's insistent theme, which overlaps the chapters, is the inter-relationship between vampires and cinema itself, in part the result of the date of publication of the vampire ur-text, Bram Stoker's *Dracula* – 1897, generally considered to be the ballpark Year Zero of cinema as a mass medium. For example, he draws interesting parallels between the supernatural beings of vampire cinema and the sexually predatory 'vamps' of early melodrama, and sees in the first major film vampire Count Orlock, in F.W. Murnau's *Nosferatu* (1922), not only the origins of the cinematic vampire as we know it but 'a creature of light, shadow and cinematic trickery – which is to say that he is a technological invention' (p.82). This is really good stuff and to my mind perfect 'Short Cuts' material in that the author is taking what is commonly understood about his subject and stretching its legs – but for me he then overeggs it by working up to the claim that the 'vampire is a stand-in for the uncanniness of cinema itself' (p.89), a sweeping assertion based largely on his affection for a single text, the admittedly remarkable metafiction *Shadow of the Vampire* (2000), a fantasy directed by E. Elias Merhige about the making of *Nosferatu* that has at its centre the brilliant conceit that the actor playing Orlock, Max Schreck (played in the film by Willem Dafoe), was actually a real vampire lured to the production by Murnau (John Malkovich) by the promise that he could sup on the female lead at the end of filming.

Shadow of the Vampire also features prominently in Ken Gelder's **New Vampire Cinema**, a sort-of sequel to the same author's *Reading the Vampire* (1994). There has been a lot of undead action in the intervening years and Gelder's book does a brisk job of mapping the territory since Francis Coppola's *Bram Stoker's Dracula* (1992) a film which, like Merhige's, appears to be making the journey from relative critical neglect on release (Gelder quotes a number of hostile reviews) to canonical cornerstone, in large part for similar reasons to do with postmodern playfulness. Indeed, it would be a fairly dim-witted viewer who did not note that a central scene in Coppola's film, that of the Count's (Gary Oldman) first meeting with Mina Harker (Winona Ryder), takes place inside a cinematograph screening the films of the Lumière brothers, and Gelder states plainly that 'vampires are, and always have been, cinematic creatures, brought to life by cinema' (p.ix); but he does not appear to be arguing, like Weinstock, that the vampire and cinema itself are somehow synonymous. Instead, via studying a variety of texts from the last two decades (Gelder has to some extent the more manageable task than Weinstock as his focus is narrower, albeit informed by what has gone before), he offers a range of interpretations of the vampire in film from around the globe.

Of course, the most commercially and socially significant vampire films (or, rather, films with vampires in them) in that period have been the *Twilight* series (2008–2012) and no doubt many students will have had their interest in this area piqued by the adventures of Edward and Bella. But the series appears to present something of a problem for those writing seriously about vampire cinema, notwithstanding the quality or otherwise of the films themselves. (Having recently been exposed to them, my overriding impression is of groups of pasty-faced youths staring balefully at one another in well-appointed, airy rooms; occasionally one of them will smile meaningfully.) This uncertainty is reflected in the films' coverage in Weinstock and Gelder's books: Gelder covers *Twilight*, *New Moon* and *Eclipse* in eight pages, some of which is discussion around their industrial status as 'event movies' (which is fair enough as this is arguably the most interesting thing about them), the rest about their allusions to class and Native Americans, which, while interesting, one suspects doesn't account for their phenomenal success; for Weinstock they barely merit a mention. In part this is no doubt a reflection of timing as neither author will have seen the final two films before submitting their manuscripts. But I think the wider problem lies in their relationship to the first of Jeffrey Weinstock's guiding principles: 'The cinematic vampire is always about sex.' Famously, the *Twilight* films (and books) are very explicitly 'about' abstinence until marriage, resulting in some extremely atypical vampire behaviour. To what extent, therefore, are they 'vampire films'? Neither author addresses this question, but the scant coverage between the covers perhaps provides its own answer.

Talking of covers, *New Vampire Cinema* has an especially ugly one, apparently an enlargement of blood cells, obscured and murkily rendered. This unfortunate presentation is upheld internally, the layout extremely cramped with the text set at a size that had me booking an eye test. As the publisher at Auteur I am very conscious of the economics of printing and of chucking missiles from a glass house, but Gelder has been done a bit of a disservice by BFI/Palgrave. The layout of *The Vampire Film*, by contrast, is almost too generous but at least allows for note taking by the assiduous student (you know the one). Physical appearance aside, both of these books are to be recommended – written at a level that I'd imagine the engaged A level student would find challenging but not inaccessibly so, they complement each other nicely as a digestible entry point to a mainstay of the horror film in cinema's first century, undead and kicking in its second.

DVD reviews
Steel: A Century of Steelmaking on Film (BFI DVD,)
Neil Coombs

Steel (1945)

The BFI have released another collection of fascinating documentaries from their archives. This new double DVD box set of 20 films is the third and final set in their 'This Working Life' series. *Steel: A Century of Steelmaking on Film* follows on from the previous two box sets in the series that explored documentary film-makers' responses to the coal and shipbuilding industries. The three industries featured in the 'This Working Life' series are perhaps most notable as part of a recently vanished world, one where Britain manufactured things and men (for it is mostly men that feature in these documentaries) worked in these three deeply interconnected industries as part of a family and class-bound tradition.

Perhaps one way into these films is to consider them in relation to the topics that feature in the social realist cinema that accompanied the decline of these once all encompassing industries. In Ken Loach's *Kes* (1969), Billy's brother Jud seethes with bitter resentment at a working life underground and Billy's only real future is 'down the pit'. The steel industry had a similar all pervasive effect on the South Wales and Yorkshire communities that feature in these films. When we watch them it is impossible not to think about the craft, skill and industry that has been lost in the privatisation and subsequent dismantling of the British steel industry. Perhaps the overweening affect of these films is one of a misplaced nostalgia for a time and place that perhaps *we* wouldn't have enjoyed.

The twenty films that are included on this discs cover the period from 1901 to 1987 and subsequently there is a fairly broad range of documentary modes and style included. What struck me most about the works is the physicality of the film. I find myself looking at the quality of 16mm and 35mm celluloid and the colour processes; the ways in which they figure history as they reproduce the reality of the period from the 1940s through to the 1960s. The tangible nature of film as an analogue medium parallels the physicality of the industry. The highlight of the set in terms of the cinematography is the restored version of Jack Cardiff's *Steel* (1945). Watching the films in one sitting there are many shots of crucibles, furnaces and flowing rivers of steel but it is Jack Cardiff's camerawork that shines out amongst the group of films. Cardiff is acknowledged as one of cinema's most important colour cinematographers, particularly his work with Powell and Pressburger (*A Matter of Life and Death* [1946], *Black Narcissus* [1947] and *The Red Shoes* [1948]). In *Steel*, red hot slag pours onto mountainous slag heaps in daylight, smoke and fire below from the furnaces, and the use of colour throughout is stunning. The score composed by Hubert Clifford and performed by the London Symphony Orchestra adds an emotional depth to the stunning cinematography.

Other films in the set include *Men of Consett* (1959): a strange anthropological study of the town in County Durham, in which Tom Stobart, a peculiar limping explorer (he had been shot while on expedition in Ethiopia and had filmed Hilary's 1953 Everest expedition) examines the life in the town, the men and 'girls' who work there. There is a particular focus on how the men can fit in their beers around their shifts as Stobart visits the pubs of Consett. Another interesting piece is the animated *River of Steel* (1951), which is one of the few films that attempts to operate in a poetic mode. The animation and colour transfers marvelously to DVD and its depiction of a world without steel is wonderfully realized. But I can imagine my students would struggle to engage with many of the films on these two discs due to their rather dry subject matter. A film such as *The Building of the New Tyne Bridge* (1928), for example, is a fascinating exploration of the type of engineering feat that we take for granted and it is quite amazing to see the men digging the riverbed from within a pressurised cylinder. What is missing from the majority of these paeans to the steel industry is any exploration of the physical toll that the work must have taken on the men and women who worked in these infernal places or any exploration of the class tensions that must surely have existed.

There is a real lack of films outside of the expository 'voice-of-god' mode and one almost wishes that the voice-over can be removed (as it can, for example, in the BFI's DVD release of Patrick Keiller's *Robinson in Ruins*). The silent films from the 1920s with their newly commissioned music by Newcastle-based band Jazzfinger demonstrate the powerful effect that a carefully composed contemporary score can have on early cinema. It would be interesting to see the documentary footage on these discs re-scored and re-imagined along the lines of Bill Morrison's elegy to the coal industry, *Miner's Hymns* (2010).

The BFI have released a range of thematic documentary sets over recent years, their output covering the rail industry, three volumes on the GPO Film Unit and five volumes of films from the Central Office of Information (running to 1500 minutes for this collection alone). But it is difficult to think how this particular set could be used in an educational environment outside of a very specialised study. The films could be used to illustrate the move from early actualities such as *His Majesty's Visit to the Clyde* (1917) to educational and expository documentaries, but there are other BFI sets with a broader range of film styles (and topics). The films are probably most interesting for colleges that are situated in the heart of the steel-making communities that feature in the films. If you are teaching Film Studies in Newcastle, Consett or Ebw Vale, then these may well be the films for you. They are indeed fascinating portraits of a vanishing world.

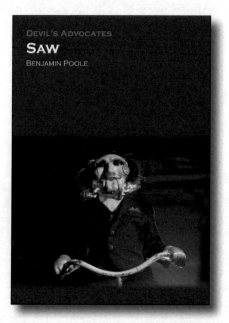

"this book had me completely hooked from beginning to end and eager to share it with colleagues and students... this seemingly little book could easily become a core text for the whole 'A' level course, being packed with everything we might need to teach.
Media Education Association"

Top down: scenes from Steve McQueen's Hunger

If There's Only One Film You Use, Make it... Hunger

by Rona Murray

Hunger (2008) is a critically-acclaimed British film, made by artist Steve McQueen about the hunger strikes by IRA prisoners interred in Long Kesh prison in Belfast over a period from 1980 to 1981. Previous (and continuing) protests (such as being 'on the blanket' – where prisoners refuse to wear the prison-issued clothes) had failed to win the prisoners the reinstatement of political status they asked for. Bobby Sands, the central figure in the group and also to *Hunger*, was the first hunger striker to die as a result of his actions. Thereafter, nine further men would die before the hunger strike ended, with no political status forthcoming. McQueen's film raises a number of key questions about choices in film form and film content, as well as marking the emergence of a new, important British film-maker.

Northern Ireland and 'The Troubles'

For his first feature, McQueen chose a still highly-charged historical story, not least because the legacy of 'The Troubles' – the name for the period between 1968 and 1997 where there was perpetual unrest, involving terrorist and official violence – is a history that is still painfully visible in Northern Ireland today. The intense hatreds revealed through the action of remembrance of the Protestant Orange Order marches, and the recent (2013) responses to a change in arrangements for flying the Union Flag, demonstrate that the sectarian divisions that fuelled the conflict have not disappeared, or in some parts hardly diminished. Only recently, in June 2010 following a further inquiry, has the British Prime Minister formally apologised for the killings on Bloody Sunday, an event that took place in 1972. Moreover, as regards Irish history, there is a further self-reflexive debate about the role of history and remembrance in the national consciousness, with an urgency engendered by the violence that the rituals of sectarian memory still threaten.[1] To make a film, therefore, about the Irish troubles of 1981 is literally to make a contemporary drama.

In preparing this article, this writer has been conscious again of the power of language (written, in this case) to define and determine a political position in relation to Northern Ireland. For example, what were the hunger strikers – political prisoners, terrorists, murderers, freedom fighters? How far should the positions 'Republican' and 'Unionist' be assumed to equate to 'Catholic' and 'Protestant'? Should the area of Belfast where the civil rights marches took place be referred to as Derry / Londonderry (the respective Republican and Unionist names at the time)? Remembering this in studying the film should remind students that language can carry a political or ideological point of view. One of the key debates students can – and should – engage in is considering the question of how the film-maker's aesthetic choices contains a political viewpoint and how it reflects these deeply divided positions. Is this a film that favours either a Republican or a Unionist point of view? More widely, what is the purpose of a film made about these historical events now? Does it pertain to situations relating to terrorism and imprisonment in our so-called post 9/11 world? Is the film asking us to focus on purely narrow, political messages? Or is it asking larger, more philosophical questions, through the medium of this story? Does it succeed in doing that?

Images of 'The Troubles'

As a modern conflict, the violence in Northern Ireland has provided many images, both still and moving, which capture and crystallise the apparent events – and crystallise people's emotions in seeing them. Thinking about the time, 1968, we can relate this to the Vietnam War (often referred to as the first 'television' war). In this period, violence happening elsewhere could be brought into people's homes via television news and reportage photographs in the newspapers.

This is directly relevant to the beginnings of the modern conflict in the province (recognising that the roots of discord stretch back into much deeper Irish history). McKittrick and McVea, in *Making Sense of The Troubles*, describe the march through the city of Derry / Londonderry in October 1968 which descended into violence:

> Crucially, a Dublin television cameraman was on hand to capture the RUC [Northern Ireland's official police force] actions on film. In particular he recorded the scene as a senior RUC officer uninhibitedly used a long blackthorn stick, the official symbol of his authority, to rain heavy blows indiscriminately on a number of marchers. The pictures of the officer fiercely laying about the demonstrators, then turning towards the camera, wild-eyed and almost out of control, were shown repeatedly at the time. In the years that followed the film clip was broadcast on television hundreds and perhaps thousands of times... (2001: 41)

The same kind of powerful, disturbing images remain from the events of Bloody Sunday, where on 30 January 1972 British paratroopers (part of the British army presence in Northern Ireland) shot dead thirteen people, and wounded fourteen, who were taking part in a civil rights march. Paul Greengrass' 2002 film, *Bloody Sunday*, uses a documentary-style aesthetic to tell the story from the participants' point of view, both marchers and soldiers. Made in a period where the families of the dead and wounded were still seeking justice for the cover-up that took place after the killings, the film is clear about where its sympathies lie. It casts the amiable figure of James Nesbitt as Ivan Cooper, the local MP who was involved in organising the march, following him prior to the events and as he deals with the aftermath. The soldiers (played by Tim Piggott-Smith and Nicholas Farrell with public schoolboy vocal authority) are representatives of the British ruling classes. Aileen Blaney, in writing on the film speaks of how it has 'spectacularised the past' in bringing to fictional life that traumatic historical event for its television (and cinema) audience. In doing so, the images on screen directly reference the photographic images taken at the time – an emotive repetition (in line with the previously-discussed image from 1968) designed to maintain the argument for justice. Its documentary style is also a reminder that this is not a film made for the purposes of entertainment; i.e. its aesthetics are important to demonstrate its sincerity and seriousness.

How is McQueen's film bound to be different from Greengrass'? One crucial element is removed for McQueen – there can be no appeal to a public, shared knowledge through visible photographic or moving images. His film is concerned with events that were hidden from public view, taking place inside Long Kesh prison in Belfast. 'Real' images are almost non-existent. Sean O'Hagan, in reviewing the film on its release for *The Observer*, refers to the '90-second snatch of film' which is the only one known to exist showing prisoner conditions inside the 'H-blocks'. He comments that it was 'shot by an Ulster Television camera crew for a documentary that was subsequently banned by the government. It shows two prisoners, bedraggled and Christ-like, wrapped in dirty blankets, shouting out their demands from a filthy, excrement encrusted cell' (O'Hagan: 2008).

O'Hagan goes on to note how an artist, Richard Hamilton, created a portrait (called 'The Citizen') from that briefly available picture. Art, his comment suggests, stepped in where reporting and documentary failed to enter. Decades later, McQueen's film is a similar, rare attempt to 'spectacularise the past' – one hidden from view literally as well as by the passage of time and forgetfulness.

What does exist in the public domain is the iconic image Long Kesh prison itself, known also as The Maze, and its particular design of H blocks (so-called because of their ground pattern in aerial photographs). Resonating with modern pictures of the prison complex at Guantanamo Bay, this building structure is peculiar to look at in photographs because of its persistence in what it does *not* reveal on repeated viewing; images of both Long Kesh and Guantanamo are symbolic of a system that creates places where actions take place (in our name) but which are hidden from our view.

What films such as McQueen's do, therefore, is to bring to life aspects of a historical story that have remained unavailable to our public scrutiny. Whereas *Bloody Sunday* animates the iconic images (from news reportage photographs), *Hunger* gives a concrete, visual reality to something that has only previously existed in journalistic phrases – 'dirty protest', 'blanket protest', 'hunger-strike', etc.

This can be seen to liberate, as well as constrain, the possibilities for McQueen in the choices he makes. Unlike a film with material already available, such as *Bloody Sunday*, McQueen can – and has – decided to strike away any suggestions of precise authenticity to the events of the time by using what we could call a more avant-garde style. Importantly, the conscious artfulness restructures a different thematic relationship with its audience – arguably suggesting that we should focus more widely than on 'the Irish question' and suggesting the film can be considered from a position larger than socially and historically situated and focussed narratives. McQueen's emphasis seems to be on the experience of the different groups trapped within a dehumanising system of corridors, who all ultimately suffer from the violence created in that melting pot. He does this particularly effectively, using a visceral specificity of physical experience to engage us as if in the present, and so ceasing to construct these individuals as historical celebrities or cyphers for social types of that era.

Establishing Empathy

This aspect of film form is useful to examine; i.e. the way in which the action of *Hunger* is grounded in the everyday. McQueen's focus on the detail of the everyday lives – of the prison warders and of the prisoners – anchors his representation in something very affecting in that it is recognisably human.

We watch as an unidentified middle-aged man sits at the dinner table, eating a fairly uninspiring meal, listening to the radio in the background. The wallpaper and the textiles (particularly his shirt's nylon appearance) are immediately recognisable to those of us old enough to remember this period. For those who are not, the flat lighting and the thin textures connote the drab and dreary environment (matched by the man's weary facial expressions). It recalls the detail used in other films, such as *This is England* (2006) or *An Education* (2009). Annette Kuhn, writing on the 'performances of memory' that take place in visual media texts (such as film and photographs) identifies the memory film, often autobiographical, which stage the process of remembering in its (in her words) 'imagistic quality that aligns it more closely to unconscious productions like dreams and fantasies than to, say, written story' (Kuhn: 2002). Whilst McQueen's film is not an autobiographical one directly, in the way the two films mentioned above are, it certainly captures something of the feeling Kuhn suggests through the fragmentary montage that McQueen drops us – unprepared, unconscious – into. The ordinariness of the scene is powerful when shot in a mode which mimics the fragmentary operation of our own memories.

The film provides ample material of the daily lives of those involved and there are narrative strands to follow in relation to Raymond Lohan (Stuart Marshall) – the prison warder – and Davey Gillen (Brian Milligan). In both story strands, we see them as people first (Lohan's role as a prison warder slowly emerges through the opening sequence – even later his role in the violence) and political cyphers second. Bobby Sands (Michael Fassbender) is not introduced until around 26 minutes into the film. The detail of their lives – the sandwich foil, the quiet cigarette (Lohan) or playing with the fly, 'dressing' the cell walls (Gillen) – are the way the film language builds these characters, placing the audience in an observational mode (with little dialogue typical for character exposition). Of course, these are details that come to have political meanings as the film progresses, but they are intensely 'real' in terms of being recognisable and relateable. An argument states that Lohan is shown to be as much of a victim of the violence as the others – culminating in his eventual assassination at his mother's nursing home. McQueen here, as elsewhere, makes use of an oblique 'Pieta' reference – Lohan's lifeless head rests in the lap (once more a child) of his mother. This, however, contrasts tellingly with images of Sands as he declines, more closely related to the traditional 'Pieta' image. And these are important moments visually to illustrate the switch from the more 'local' narrative of the H block protests to a consideration of the wider, more philosophical implications of this story. As the Chief Medical Officer (Billy Clarke) lifts and cradles the emaciated figure, it is the act of compassion by this carer which is the focus now, and it moves the debate beyond the political.

All three strands offer different narrative perspectives. We enter the prison through the eyes of Lohan and Gillen. At the end, we look from it through the eyes of Sands (and his boyhood reveries). A question remains – which of these has proved powerful enough emotionally to determine our feelings? This will, effectively, determine our position through our emotional responses to the politics, unless we consider the film to be beyond the local history and aiming for a much larger meditation on humanity and our relationships to each other. Its form as a kind of 'art' film suggests that the latter is the case. An interesting moment to analyse might be our response to the Loyalist orderly who allows Sands to fall as he struggles out of the bath. Is this to be read as a narrow political point by the film-maker by this stage in the narrative? It is this orderly we clearly see carry Sands back in his arms in the subsequent shots.

This is not to deny its political effect on audiences who remember the history directly. When Lohan (nameless in the film itself, significantly) moves outside to his car, his sudden movement (dropping down to check underneath the vehicle) is immediately recognisable. This moment arguably moves that personal identification into something that Kuhn described where the individual gives way to an act of memory that has 'social and cultural, as well as personal, resonance' (Kuhn: 2010: 298). This action of checking for bombs underneath the car is a small detail, which metonymically stands for that Northern Irish history of violence. In terms of audience reception, McQueen's film (made by a mainland Brit) provides a different experience for the mainland audience than for an Irish one. Sukhdev Sandhu, reviewing the film in the *Daily Telegraph*, comments how the film is 'a visceral and vitally important reawakening of repressed memories'. Is it, therefore, possible to argue that the film is able to act as an intervention – anew – in reminding a British audience of a story that was hidden away from view, through the signs that existed publically? This involves explaining the history to young students, but it is an important aspect of the film's power.

Hunger as an Art Film

By comparison, in many of the reviews, there is an emphasis on the non-political nature of McQueen's film as a result of its form. These are worth considering in the light of the above but most importantly used as comparisons to the students' impressions and analysis having watched the film. Is it an 'art film' first and foremost?

A useful starting point for discussion may be these extended quotes from British newspaper reviews:

> A friend of mine from Northern Ireland, who has seen *Hunger*, said McQueen had 'pulled off the impossible' by 'making an art film about the IRA'. When I mention the term 'art film', McQueen throws me a fierce look. 'I don't know what you mean by that,' he says. 'What I tried to do was make the strongest, most powerful film I could from the events and the story. It may not have the conventional narrative of most feature films but that is my way of grappling with the subject. Art has absolutely nothing to do with it. (O'Hagan: 2008)

Without taking sides or sanctifying terrorism, he successfully plunges us into the psychological landscapes of the early 1980s, demonstrating not only an artist's flair for framing and for isolating telling features and details, but a genius for dramatic set-pieces that's worthy of mid-70s Scorsese. *Hunger* is breeze-block heavy, an unforgettable portrait of battered and self-battering masculinity... (Sandhu: 2008)

The following are simply suggestions of aspects of film language that students could use to consider this further:

- Aspects of Film Form – visual and sound
  In discussing the film as an art film, the reviewers clearly engage with the non-conventional use of film form adopted by McQueen. This includes images of the prison cells after they are subject to the 'dirty protest' – the excrement forming beautiful patterns of swirls and whorls (ones which the prison officer brought into clean them takes a moment to observe – perhaps admire). Reviewers pointed to the film's apparently conscious references to Western art (e.g. Rembrandt, in particular).[2] Other aspects to consider is the centred stillness which envelops the film for much of its running time – non-diegetic music is rarely used, the only striking occurrence being the ambient soundtrack to accompany Sands' fantasy of running as boy through the crow-filled trees at the end of the film. There are snatches of dialogue, rather than extended conversations, which serves to emphasise the lengthy central debate between Sands and Father Dominic Moran (Liam Cunningham) as a turning point and a point at which all narrative is suspended. What are the effects of these, and other, film form choices on the way in which we view this narrative? Importantly, students can consider whether it is McQueen's intention to make an 'art film' (perhaps because of his background), or ask whether that particular film language serves a purpose in the narrative.

- Dramatic Set Pieces
  A shocking sequence involves the prisoners running the gamut of riot police, brought into the prison, where they are beaten and subjected to violent, invasive physical examinations by the guards. It is a scene that affected McQueen badly, because the physical contact needed to be real; his role in orchestrating that genuine violence became understandably unbearable. The sequence offers us a further narrative perspective, as we enter the prison alongside a riot officer Stephen Graves (Ben Peel) who is clearly intimidated by his prospective role. The prisoners' naked bodies – emphasising further their Christ-like subjection to faceless, brutal authority – are passed through in a sequence where the usual contemplative silence is broken by a cacophony of noise, shouting and beating. McQueen is very clear about the statement contained here – Graves (only identified by name in the credits) breaks down as a result of his participation. The image joins that of Lohan leaning against the wall or bathing his hands – there is nothing triumphalist about these men's experiences of administering 'justice' behind closed walls. This is where the film, most affectively, examines the nature of empathy as part of its apparently wider, philosophical concerns. Not just a film about Northern Irish politics, but

one which considers man's inhumanity to man in these systems of control and punishment behind walls. As Roger Ebert, critic of the *Chicago Sun Times*, states:

If you do not hold a position on the Irish Republican cause, you will not find one here. *Hunger* is not about the rights and wrongs of the British in Northern Ireland, but about the inhumane prison conditions, the steeled determination of IRA members like Bobby Sands, and a rock and a hard place. (Ebert, 2009)

Bobby Sands – Model of Matyrdom?

Audiences' responses to Bobby Sands may be deeply coloured by their knowledge of or cultural position at the time of the hunger strikes. Mainland responses, as explored above, could be characterised more as an ignorance of what was happening (day to day) behind the prison walls (an aspect McQueen comments on from his own experience). In the course of recovering this history, McQueen and Enda Walsh (his co-screenwriter) construct a potentially very traditional narrative of Sands' martyrdom. Looking at the history of these kinds of representation in Ireland, Guy Beiner (2007) refers to a 'model of martyrdom' that draws on a 'triumph of defeat', perpetuated in public memory through 'countless hagiographic histories and street ballads'. Does McQueen's film contribute to that tradition?

The film's central (22 and a half minute) conversation between Sands and Father Moran, for which all the action is suspended, argues out the existential rights and wrongs of dying for a cause and actually presents some of those ideas of martyrdom to critical scrutiny. Although there is an intense romanticism in the treatment of Sands' boyhood story, McQueen attempts to make sense of the nature of martyrdom itself. Moran challenges Sands' determination to die. The film's thematic emphasis is on the wider discourse relating to the personal decisions to be made within that rigid system – and the clear implication that all participants take on the responsibility for their own (Sands included).

There is also, in the way in which this debate acts as a narrative turning point, a suggestion from the film. Once all the arguments have been worked through – on both sides – what is left? There is a strong emphasis in the representation of Sands' decline that it is the acts of gentleness and humanity (as discussed above,) rather than dehumanisation caused by intransigent beliefs, that are the most affective, particularly in the narrative's late stages.

Prison Images: Long Kesh and Guantanamo Bay

Do the ideas behind *Hunger* have anything in common with how we encounter ideas of Guantanamo Bay or the situation of prisoners in the so-called 'War on Terror'? Steve McQueen comments on the DVD extras that he did not have a fully distinct knowledge of the situation of the Irish prisoners as a child growing up on the mainland. Additionally, 'The Troubles' were a war being waged nearby but distinctly culturally 'somewhere else'. Reports of its violence entered teatime homes just as reports from Afghanistan and Iraq do now and with a similar sense pervading of a hopeless war from which a resolution was unlikely to be found.

In fact, there is substantial difference in the way in which these two places are 'spectacularised', not least because of the different eras in which they exist. Susan Sontag writes on the effect of seeing behind the walls of Abu Ghraib. In an article (2004) published in the *New York Times* concerning these photographs, she argues that Western memory is now a visual one. These photographs, and how their impact can be sustained through the repetition inherent in digital media, have let us in on that impregnated mystery behind the prison walls – of man's (and woman's) capacity for inhumanity and abuse of power in torture. Sontag denotes the pictures as – contrary to President Bush's assertion – really part of the 'true nature and heart of America'; i.e. in Sontag's view, a nation that not only engages in brutality but has no shame in exporting images of it. As memory is being constantly remediated through changing technologies, the availability of digital media ensures, in her words, a 'hall of mirrors' in the endless capacity for re-publication. Sontag's polemic concludes that it is 'unstoppable'. Although, in the early 1980s, we did not see into the heart of the regime in place inside the Maze, apart from occasional (smuggled) images of the prisoners in rather strange, posed (almost casual snapshot) attitudes, we *have* now apparently seen into the heart of darkness in the American forces carrying out the imperialist task.

Sontag here, as elsewhere, accents the ethical/moral dimension of photography; its ability to reveal a truth that ruling elites would prefer was keep hidden. McQueen, albeit in the moving image rather than still photographic ones, shares this impetus towards the moral. His film, formed in the same cultural moment of the Abu Ghraib atrocities, finds the artist questioning the action of a political moment – the clash of ideological extremes – that causes a man to be prepared to give his life. His film enters the current dialectic – post the Ghraib images – by offering a further understanding of the marginalised figure of the terrorist (reclaimed from behind Margaret Thatcher's famous statement, 'Murder is murder is murder') who might have perpetrated terrible wrongs but is still deserving of treatment higher than that of animals. As the film widens the debate to individual and collective responsibility for humanity, our modern selves and, for some of us, our 1980s selves are counterpointed.

The force of this might allow comparing the film with the German cultural mindset of *vergangenheitbewältstigung* – the coming to terms with your national, cultural past – a form of memory work necessarily forced upon the German consciousness as a result of the Nazi regime and the horrors carried out in the name of the German people. McQueen's film is a coming to terms with the past on the part of a collective social group. *Hunger* is a form of political intervention to the extent that British mainland audiences have been able to remain in a state of forgetting, or dis-remembrance of, as McQueen himself puts it, 'the history in our own backyard'. *Hunger*, through the form of film, remediates and reactivates that buried memory powerfully on an *individual* level – arguably in a way that can animate social memory at a collective level (with enough force that one French critic suggested that it should be called *Anger*, not *Hunger*).

Steve McQueen

Steve McQueen is a British artist, winner of the Turner prize in 1999, born and raised in London. Prior to *Hunger*, he had produced several films as part of his art installation work. He attended Tisch School in New York to study film, but did not complete (he has commented variously on the restrictions there). A related work to *Hunger* is his piece *Queen and Country*, commissioned as the official war artist for the Imperial War Museum. This moveable exhibition (it has travelled around the UK) consisted of panels containing the images of soldiers who had died in Iraq and Afghanistan, rendered as a sheet of Royal Mail postage stamps. McQueen's stated intention was, in fact, to have the images commissioned onto actual stamps, stating: 'The stamps would focus on individual experience without euphemism. It would form an intimate reflection of national loss that would involve the families of the dead and permeate the everyday – every household and every office.'[3] This is particularly relevant since permeating events into the everyday, filtering their wider importance through the visceral experience of everyday routines, is the aesthetic choice made in *Hunger*, one which initiates the action of personal memory as a powerful aid to awakening our response to its themes.

The film-maker Steve McQueen is important in this because he begins as an artist – but an artist who has a clear interest in the political role of art. However, it is the acts of gentleness and humanity, rather than dehumanisation caused by intransigent beliefs, which are the most affective, particularly in the narrative's late stages. Here, the personal reasserts itself amongst the political. McQueen's aesthetic makes from scratch a world he does not know and, as a member of the 'imperialist' majority, there is no impetus to re-examine the event to counteract the experience of trauma as one of the victims; or to reimagine the past as part of the current political debate. However, the action of the film's narrative dialectic is, I would argue, to re-energise the political relevance of the hunger strikes as regards our current relationship to extremism.

In *Hunger*, McQueen's choice of aesthetics is important in removing conventional film language devices used to cue emotional responses in the audience. Just as Greengrass considered a documentary aesthetic appropriate to telling the events of Bloody Sunday, McQueen has chosen an aesthetic that seeks to convey the powerful emotion of the situation, its emotional reality. In this case, it is created using the signifiers of an 'art film' style (e.g. the stillness, the lack of traditional cause and effect motion of the plot, absence of diegetic music).

To finish, let's consider McQueen as a film-maker. Can we detect elements of a signature style here? *Shame* (2011) represents a distinct step-change from the historical events of *Hunger* and it would be specious to draw too firm a comparison between the two films and to impose an 'auteurist' interpretation on his output. An audience member at the Cornerhouse, Manchester Q&A session for *Shame* suggested that both films were concentrated on the themes of how humanity is lost (in H block or in sex addiction) and the working out of this on the human body, including the (different) political implications of each of these.[4] In both, there is a question of the voyeurism in observing these extremes of experience on screen. Still, perhaps the variety of McQueen's work (including his installations) should counsel against insisting on shoehorning his work into the 'auteur' shaped space. He has, anyway, been referred to as part of a 'golden age' of British film-making in a newspaper article by Andrew Pulver in 2011. Pulver makes an interesting argument that, for the first time in a long time, the scope of British films and film-makers requires 'actual categorisation' – a change, he argues, from the occasional, high-profile success story. McQueen appears in his article in a group of 'furrowed brows and intense discussions' which 'betray the art-movie mavens' whilst elsewhere more commercial directors hang out. The article also highlights the funding conditions (under the now defunct UK Film Council) which seemed to give birth to a rich variety of films and creative imaginations, and that curious British discourse that classifies the commercial separate from the artistic. In fact, whatever the future holds in terms of British film-making supported in Britain, McQueen is clearly able to spread his funding wings away from British models (public television, regional aid and direct public finance) to attract private American money for his latest feature, *Twelve Years a Slave*. Currently in post-production, it has a star-laden cast and in one case, star and producer in Brad Pitt (with his Plan B Entertainment company backing the feature). This may erode a romantic narrative for McQueen's film-making as a marginal, avant-garde or part of a peculiarly British art cinema style. It may be exactly the means to maintain the work of a film-maker whose aesthetics so far seem to be the servant of the story not its master signature.

Some Suggested Areas for Discussion

- What is the effect of McQueen's choice of film language in *Hunger*?
- How does it compare to the choices made by Paul Greengrass in *Bloody Sunday*?
- How might different audiences respond to this film? For example, older compared to younger audiences? Republican compared to Unionist? As an audience member, do you need to know the relevant history to engage and appreciate the film?
- In what way is the film shocking or extreme? Identify specific features of film language McQueen uses to ensure it makes an impact on the audience.
- What do the difficulties in placing the film into a category – such as genre, authorship – tell you about its construction?
- How would you, using a film like *Hunger*, characterise the features of an 'art film'?

Resources

Beiner, Guy (2007) 'Between Trauma and Triumphalism: The Easter Rising, the Somme, and the Crux of Deep Memory in Modern Ireland.' *The Journal of British Studies*. Vol 46 (2), pp.366-389.

Blaney, Aileen (2007) 'Remembering Historical Trauma in Paul Greengrass's *Bloody Sunday*'. *History and Memory*, Volume 19, No2, Fall/Winter 2007, pp.113-138.

Brown, Mark (2010) 'Artist Steve McQueen fights on to put Britain's war dead on stamps' in *The Guardian*, 18 March 2010. http://www.guardian.co.uk/artanddesign/2010/mar/18/steve-mcqueen-iraq-soldiers-stamps

Ebert, Roger (2009) '*Hunger* – Reviews'. *Chicago Sun Times*. 15 April 2009. http://rogerebert.suntimes.com/apps/pbcs.dll/article?AID=/20090415/REVIEWS/904159995

Kuhn, Annette (2002) *Family Secrets: Acts of Memory and Imagination*, Brooklyn, NY: Verso.

McKittrick, David and David McVea (2001) *Making Sense of The Troubles*, London: Penguin.

O'Hagan, Sean (2008) 'McQueen and Country'. *The Guardian*. 12 October 2008. http://www.guardian.co.uk/film/2008/oct/12/2

Pulver, Andrew (2011) 'British cinem'as golden age is now'. *The Guardian*. 13 October 2011.

Rolston, Bill (2010) 'Trying to reach the future through the past: Murals and Memory in Northern Ireland.' *Crime Media Culture*. Volume 6(3) pp.285-307.

Sandhu, Sukhdev (2008) '*Hunger* – review'. *The Daily Telegraph* 31 October 2008. http://www.telegraph.co.uk/culture/film/filmreviews/3562731/Hunger-by-Steve-McQueen-review.html

Sontag, Susan (2004) 'Regarding the Torture of Others.' *The New York Times*, 23 May 2004.

Films and Art Works

Bloody Sunday (2002) (Dir: Paul Greengrass. Prod: Irish Film Board/Granada Television)

Shame (2011) (Dir: Steve McQueen. Prod: See-Saw Films/Film 4/UK Film Council)

Twelve Years a Slave (post-production). (Dir: Steve McQueen. Prod: New Regency Entertainment/Plan B/River Road)

Queen and Country. Artwork by Steve McQueen:
http://www.artfund.org/queenandcountry/Queen_and_Country.html

Footnotes

1. See, for example, Rolston (2010).
2. See Jonathan Jones: http://www.guardian.co.uk/artanddesign/ jonathanjonesblog/2008/nov/20/steve-mcqueen-hunger-rembrandt-art
3. As of 2010, newspapers reported that McQueen was still campaigning for the stamps, with the families' backing. See http://www.guardian.co.uk/ artanddesign/2010/mar/18/steve-mcqueen-iraq-soldiers-stamps
4. As a tangential point, much has been made about the performance of the body in these films, by their lead actor (Michael Fassbender, both times). For *Hunger*, this meant his loss of 40 pounds to play the emaciated Sands.

Studying British Cinema: 1999–2009

John Fitzgerald

In Volume VII issue 1 of *Splice*

𝕿𝖍𝖊 𝕿𝖎𝖒 𝕭𝖚𝖗𝖙𝖔𝖓 𝖎𝖘𝖘𝖚𝖊

The best writing for teachers and students on one of contemporary cinema's most enduring and consistently popular figures.

Available Summer 2013